EXECUTIVE WIVES

EXECUTIVE WIVES

How to Become the Powerful Influence
behind Successful Men

Wendy Walden
with Julie Chrystyn

MERCURY

First published in 1991
by Mercury Books
Gold Arrow Publications Limited,
862 Garratt Lane, London SW17 0NB

Set in Palatino by
Phoenix Photosetting, Chatham, Kent
Printed and bound in Great Britain by
Mackays of Chatham PLC, Chatham, Kent

British Library Cataloguing in Publication Data

Walden, Wendy
   Executive wives: How to become the powerful influence behind successful men.
   I. Title   II. Chrystyn, Julie
   650.1082

ISBN 1-85251-100-1

This book is dedicated to my beloved husband who has always supported me in everything I wanted to do.

Contents

Foreword

I have written this book in order to share with my readers that which I teach in my courses. My aim is to assist those women who, in this age of the nineties, enjoy the valuable role of supporting their husbands towards achieving their success.

Because corporate wives are now an integral part of our business lives, my objective is to ensure that if we wish to take up this activity, we do it as well as we possibly can!

By writing the book, I hope it will reach those wives who would like to know more about the role of a company wife, but who perhaps do not wish to participate in seminar work.

Wendy Walden

1

How it all began

That feeling of rising uneasiness was creeping upon me again. I recognised all the symptoms: feverish head, icy limbs, an increased heart rate, the tensing up of shoulder and neck muscles. For a moment all went black followed by blurry vision. I sat down, grabbed hold of the armrest and inhaled deeply. I wasn't prepared to deal with the situation one more time.

No, it wasn't the onset of a coronary attack or an epileptic seizure I was experiencing, but rather rising panic at the role I was obliged to perform that evening as hostess to a group of my husband's colleagues and their spouses in the medical profession. The idea appeared about as desirable then as a weekend in Baghdad would be following the Gulf War. However, with my husband riding high in the business social circuit, I thought of myself as the sacrificial mate at his side who would wither gracefully.

As my fixed gaze penetrated through the window on that rainy, grey Bristol afternoon, I thought of another evening devoid of adventure, mission, vitality or ideas. I wondered if the dress I had chosen for the evening was appropriate. I wondered if I would be up to conversation on current issues or medical news . . . I glanced at my watch. Three hours to go. Another deep sigh told me the situation was in control of me and not vice versa. Unlike potential winners, when faced with a challenge I did not translate the task into ways that allow positive and effective action.

As my husband's medical practice grew increasingly success-ful and he became an active member and sometimes leader of our community, he fully expected me to 'perform' flawlessly, enthusiastically and, above all, successfully while at his side. To complicate matters further, on occasion I was even called upon to speak or entertain on his behalf. I was to be the silver-tongued hostess, combining brains, charm and irreverent wit in a potent brew that would be irresistible to his colleagues, their spouses, members of the business community, charity fund-raisers and sometimes even the local press.

That translated into a tall order for one who did not apply for the job while saying 'I do' at the altar. I struggled through the functions every time. I found it very difficult indeed to make conversation with men, but even more with women. So many of the wives seemed to have so much more than me to offer. They had interests. Some had careers. These women were able to converse on so many topics. So, I found myself intimidated into a hopeless silence, caught in a quagmire of bewilderment and loss. What a bore I must have been!

No, I was not someone with an intense desire to seize the maximum advantage out of what appeared to be the reductive triviality of events. Instead, I hunted for excuses not to go and was mercifully relieved if one of my ruses worked. 'The children were ill.' 'I was ill.' 'I was too tired.' Any excuse at all as long as I was not put through that torment and be led to such a total feeling of inadequacy. At times, I was engulfed with fear. Each evening I would arrive nearly paralysed with terror. My husband, quite rightly, would circulate among the guests and leave me to do the same. I would practise for hours on end during the day what I would say and how would I say it, but when I was actually face to face with other guests, my mind went blank.

The worst ordeals of all were those occasions when my husband presided over an organisation and I was expected to appear on his behalf at a social function. As president's wife, I was obliged to sit at the top table. The trauma I experienced was much the same as of those on death row awaiting execution. I would inevitably be seated next to someone I had never met, who was considerably older than me, and – to make matters worse – a professional man. I would desperately try to make conversation, but by the end of the evening I was predictably exhausted and felt a complete failure. Anyone, I thought, any-one who would feel good afterwards would probably also enjoy train wrecks or maybe a day at the beach watching an oil slick wash ashore.

Each morning after such an evening, I would go through most of it over and over again in my mind. Why couldn't I cope with the problem? I tried to resolve this mystery endlessly. I was reasonably well educated. I grew up in a professional environment. I had interests and amusing friends. So why, then, did I have this unreasonable fear? Could I have been responsible for the disintegration of my actions? In this respect, my experience resembled that of sufferers of depression: negative thoughts, feeling miserable and having difficulty doing things.

In hindsight, this time of my life was the turning-point. I was determined to change, to make a success of this situation for my husband as well as for myself. Turbulence and trouble occasionally make for necessary evolution.

Over the next few months, I planned a campaign. Not knowing whether it would work, I plotted my strategy and was determined to give it a try. It was a humble course of action in comparison with what I now do for others professionally, but at that time my nerve was all I had to go on. So, I slogged some heavily travelled ground. I began by changing my thought patterns. 'I can't do it' became 'I can do it' in my mind. I started thinking of a whole variety of positive qualities I possessed. The challenge had to be met head-on. I knew that each action completed would be accompanied by some self-congratulation. This, in itself, would begin to produce a more positive self-image.

So I began to study other people at all the social functions I attended. In fact, I became a shrewd observer of people and their interactive style at every social gathering I was a part of, whether large or small. I would endeavour to establish what made *them* interesting, how they coped with seemingly difficult situations. The more I watched and listened, the more fascinating it became. I learned, for instance, that the best hostesses always appeared to be genuinely interested in their guests – all of them! Behind the charm, there was a professional constantly at work. They had a way of encouraging their guests to talk about themselves. The hostess made mental notes (and possibly jotted them down afterwards) regarding her guests' interests and their comments in general. At a moment's notice, she could recall

3

their remarks during future meetings. It was an instant conversation starter. 'How is your golf these days?' I could ask. 'Has Sally passed her A levels?' I once heard a woman ask a guest about her trip to New York. She said, 'New York is Calcutta without the cows,' and was truly flattered that her hostess had remembered to ask about the visit.

I vividly recall when I first tried this out for myself. I was seated next to a prominent London businessman and I took the liberty of encouraging him to tell me about himself in the manner I had seen others do. I remember that he was a tall fellow with a shock of white hair. He wore a Savile Row dark pin-striped jacket over a barrel chest. He asserted his masculinity by talking tersely and incessantly about his business, his children, his favourite sport and, yes, even his car! – His Rolls-Royce Silver Spirit II was to impress itself, himself and me. I heard of the white leather interior with navy piping, the glossy walnut dashboard, the Spirit of Ecstasy on the front! Every limb of my body grew to require medical attention as a result of severe numbness. The animated expression on my face became weary as well, but I managed to continue listening and occasionally grunt a few questions between his speaking and inhaling refuelling breaths of air. I felt like the Wimbledon champion striving to win under the most extreme psychological stress.

Much to my amazement, I found the evening went with a swing. Imagine my surprise when at the end of the evening, he said, 'Wendy, you are one of the most interesting people I have ever talked to!'

From that moment on, I went from strength to strength. Observing and listening were only the first steps of a personal strategy that skyrocketed all the way to a successful public relations career.

As time went on after the initial success of my experiment that memorable evening, I learned how to augment some of my new-found confidence by other methods as well. If confidence was the key link in the chain of success, then I was determined to acquire all parts of the sum in order to make myself as complete as possible. I learned to sound confident, look confident and ultimately feel confident. A tall order in a short statement indeed, but I have discovered since confidence became such a great motivator in my life, that all else has fallen into place more easily. I went from being a happily resigned housewife, whose only aim was to please others, to setting and accomplishing major goals for myself.

My faith in myself grew daily and although I still suffered bad days from time to time, I found that there were simply many things in life to enjoy so, I would not harp on the negative.

When my two daughters were at school all day, I felt I could work away from home and applied for a position at one of our local hotels, one of an international chain. The position I sought was to organise conferences at the hotel for companies from abroad. I thought the job would be exciting and went along to the interview wearing my bright colours, hoping I looked more confident than I felt. Imagine my surprise when a week later I learned the job was mine!

The ensuing years were some of the happiest in my life. The lessons I learned stood me in good stead. The people visiting the hotel were from all walks of life and from many countries. I enjoyed meeting them and being involved in their work. Two years passed and I was asked to head the public relations department for this hotel and, later, for the entire hotel group.

Life, it became apparent to me, is all about our approach to people – making friends, knowing business acquaintances and building business relationships.

I often recall what a friend told me in those early days. She worked as a magazine editor and constantly appeared to embrace new ideas. She would say, 'Wendy, happiness and success are not just the property of the affluent, influential and powerful. It's there for you also, but you have to believe that you deserve it. Nobody can treat you better than you treat yourself. Nobody can like you better than you like yourself. It's as simple as that! We have one shot around in this life and the sin is not the social blunder. The sin is one day wasted in self-hate; one day wasted of God's beautiful life.'

Carole always said I had to believe that I was a bundle of dynamite. 'If you don't believe it, fake it till you make it!' was her motto. 'If you don't believe it, say it before you walk into any room: I am a confident, assured, smart, beautiful woman and you're going to like me.' This reminded me of what actress Lauren Bacall would say before entering a room: 'I'm just as good as everyone else and better than most!' Did you ever see a plain, mousy-looking woman who is yet the centre of attention wherever she goes? It's the kind of woman that Helen Gurley Brown, editor of American *Cosmopolitan*, calls a 'mouseburger'. I used to wonder what made her so special. But now I know. It's because she has decided that she is the greatest thing alive. Because she thinks this, she believes it. On the other hand, did you ever see a stunningly beautiful woman sitting at the end of the table looking like a sour lemon? She accepts her lot. It's all her fault. She believes she's useless and therefore deserves to be ignored.

Having put much of this belief into practice, I stumbled upon the realisation one day that my business skills and faith in my abilities required me to break yet further new ground. So in 1978 I started my own public relations consultancy business and decided to specialise in promoting corporate individuals such as chairmen, managing directors and politicians. My work was to promote them both internally within their own companies so they developed excellent relations with their staff, and externally whereby the public could identify their company or government post through the individual. Imagine my (next) surprise when *Today* reported a decade later that I 'can take a company director and make him a potential chairman. [She] can mould a minister out of a backbencher, and create a vice-chancellor out of a professor.'

True, I have helped advance the careers of many politicians and executives. I have travelled the world over and met presidents and prime ministers, and yet nearly two decades later I am still grateful to all those friends who have helped me in the past, often unwittingly, to learn my hard-earned lessons of confidence.

Each day one still learns a little more, but life is a lot easier now, not to mention more adventurous and enjoyable. I came to believe that the root of the matter is knowing that the positive mental attitude starts with me. The world will not come and say, 'Oh, we made a mistake. We really like doormats'. It starts with me. When I began to act as though I deserved credit and respect, I got credit and respect.

So, you see, I want to share my knowledge with you for a very good reason. If you think that confidence is not for you, I want *you* to think again!

6

It was while I was involved in the specialised work of promoting executives, politicians and men of public acclaim, that I came across the 'situation' of the corporate wife. Most of my clients happen to be men and when an event warranted the inclusion of their wives, too many of the executives and politicians became grief-stricken. I heard things like, 'They don't want to participate,' or 'They hate attending company functions.' Some said, 'I would prefer not to ask my wife.' But those who were brutally honest even said things like, 'My wife is a liability. She doesn't fit in.' Unfortunately, I even heard words such as 'embarrassed', 'unsophisticated', 'uninformed' and 'not-with-the-times.'

Not to my surprise, I found that, far from not wanting to participate and support their husbands, these women lacked the confidence and enthusiasm to take part. They were being put into exactly the same position as I had been all those years ago. They were experiencing precisely the same feelings of frustration. They were despondent. To make matters worse, many of the young wives were desperate about their marraiges because of the situation. Many of the older wives resigned themselves to a quiet existence, allowing their husbands to lead separate, independent lives.

Just recently, it was with great unease that I experienced the latter. A client from London in his early sixties was on business in Los Angeles, and I flew in several days later to accompany him on a few appointments for the day. My flight arrived at 10 am on Thursday and Mr Roberts (as we shall call him) greeted me at the airport. Shortly after we said our 'hellos' to each other and proceeded through the crowded airport and into the smog-filled LA streets, Mr Roberts began to apologise.

'I hope you don't mind, Wendy,' he said with anguish in his voice, 'but I brought my wife along on this trip. I have been travelling so much lately and the poor thing has been cooped up at home. Out of guilt, I brought her along. We took a two-day holiday in San Francisco. Since we are flying back home tonight, she's with me today and waiting for us in the car.'

I certainly didn't think her presence was an intrusion of any kind and, furthermore, I resented his description of their situation. But I smiled and nodded in approval. Although Mrs Roberts and I had been introduced briefly once in the past, it was not significant enough for even an acquaintanceship. As we got into the waiting car, Mr Roberts carried on our conversation while completely ignoring the woman in the back seat. I found it necessary to turn round and greet Mrs Roberts, literally having to cut off his chatter. Again, he began explaining her presence. We drove to Beverly Hills and stopped for a quick, early lunch at Café Rodeo. Mrs Roberts was clearly uncomfortable and insisted that we carry on with business conversation and lunch, requesting only iced tea for herself.

'Dear, you must eat!' ordered Mr Roberts.

'Really, I am not hungry. Don't worry about me,' she replied.

'But you haven't eaten. You must eat, dear,' he persisted.

'I'm fine. Honestly, I'm fine,' she said.

'You won't be fine later. What would you like?' he said, losing some patience.

'Well, all right, then order me just a little something,' she said.

'What do you want?'

'Anything you order will be fine . . .'

As we sat there on the back terrace, I was somewhat perplexed and wondering if I was witnessing a scene from Abbott and Costello.

Mr Roberts lit a cigar. He offered me one. 'Later,' I said. Mrs Roberts gave me a strange look. She placed her hands under her chin and looked straight ahead. She was clearly a kind, loving, gentle woman. She wore 'sensible' shoes, a full cotton skirt with elasticised waist and a polyester/cotton short-sleeved top. Over her chair hung a cardigan as well as an all-purpose handbag. Her greying short hair was 'set' a few days ago and her lovely complexion was devoid of make-up. When I encouraged conversation, she talked about the children 'when they were younger'. I genuinely liked her, but I couldn't believe that she had been married to a very successful and wealthy businessman for more than thirty years. I felt sorry for her. I began to feel angry towards him. And I wondered if that could have been me if I had not stubbornly charted a new course in life while I still had time.

We drove a few miles down Wiltshire Boulevard just past Nieman-Marcus and the Beverly Wilshire Hotel to our first destination. He parked on the street, a rare find, and walked round to open my door. I stepped out. He shut the door and began to walk. Something is wrong here, I thought in the rush of the moment. 'What about . . .' I began asking. 'She'll wait in the car,' he said as he cut me off.

I tried to retain my composure. Our meeting lasted more than an hour. Mrs Roberts sat there waiting patiently. She did not roll down the window. I don't think she even uncrossed her legs or adjusted the cardigan hanging from her shoulders.

'Are you still here, dear?' he asked.

'Yes,' she replied, not sounding surprised at the question.

'Good,' he said.

'She certainly is a gorgeous-looking woman!' Mr Roberts remarked with great zest, commenting on the businesswoman we had just met.

'How can you tell under the mask of make-up and the mop of hair?' I said for Mrs Roberts' sake.

But he continued to extol the physical virtues of what was really an average-looking woman, to the discomfort of both Mrs Roberts and myself. The next two stops proved to be under much the same circumstances.

We arrived at the airport that evening quite exhausted, but with an extra hour till departure. Mr Roberts suggested dinner at an airport restaurant. My appetite that night threatened the share value of his company, but not to worry, Mrs Roberts ordered only coffee. Leaving her entirely out of our conversation, Mr Roberts finally turned to face her and simply offered a short 'look'. A minute later, Mrs Roberts said she really should find something for the grandchildren and exusing herself, headed for a gift shop.

'I'll leave you two to talk,' she said.

'Don't use the credit cards,' he told her.

9

He used this private time to unwind a bit, and explained why they remained married. 'She's just too nice a person to hurt,' he said, 'but she doesn't interfere in my life at all.'

I boarded the plane to Houston that evening wanting to feel elated about the success of our meeting that day, but all I could think about was Mrs Roberts' humble life. How many other women are also in her position or unknowingly on the way there? Then, I realised fully that my work with the executive wives had enormous value and I felt proud of the gigantic progress we had made.

A couple of years back, I began running a series of courses within my company for wives of top executives and politicians. At first, I saw the women on a one-to-one basis. We would explore in depth each personal problem, each personal fear. Gradually, as more and more wives indicated their wish to attend these sessions, I began to run one-day seminars for almost twenty participants at a time. The routine began by painting an overall picture of the national and international business scene and went on to describe in general terms the companies of the husbands whose wives were attending, the business situations they would or were likely to encounter and how to overcome their fears concerning those situations. We finally reviewed a reading list and advised on how to stay in touch with current affairs. Other women required guidance in social skills. Perhaps they would like to become more effective hostesses or wished to feel more at ease as guests. They might wish to sharpen conversation skills or develop an aura of charisma, energy and self-control. Yet others might require guidance with a physical reappraisal to achieve that executive style and executive look.

Overall, a woman's professional, social, intellectual and physical image should portray nothing but success. In other words, she looks as if she and her husband are worth the money! Executive wives learn about the importance of details and how details combine to create effective, impressive and powerful results. By projecting smooth corporate etiquette, she and her husband achieve spectacular business and personal success.

Just the other day, I was once again reminded of the success of this formula. One of the wives who came to see me was the wife of the managing director of a very large and well-known computer corporation. He had worked his way up from account manager to managing director in just a few years and his ambition was to become president. His wife was terrified at the thought of having to entertain clients and colleagues. She hated meeting his colleagues and their spouses because she felt inferior – simply because she was aware that most of them knew her husband had started at the company in one of the most unimportant positions.

In the beginning, I had many sessions with her to establish her confidence. Why should she feel inferior? She was and is as good as anyone else. I gave her some confidence exercises to do which we shall discuss later in the book. Then I discussed with her the art of listening and becoming interested in the people she would meet. I knew that during the summer months ahead, her husband would be entertaining a good deal with outdoor sporting events and that she should try out the exercise with the people attending these events.

1. Always smile when being introduced.

2. Ask questions about others' lives, interests, etc.

3. Make a note of their response as soon as possible.

4. Always listen intently to what is being said and appear to be genuinely interested.

She came to see me after the first event where she had to meet nearly twenty potential clients and their spouses. She systematically talked to each and every one of them, religiously following the prescribed advice. She became ecstatic as she recounted how the people were delighted to talk about themselves, while she found it relatively easy to talk with them. Later, she went on to say that when she met the same people again, she was able to approach them confidently and to talk about the things she knew they would find interesting.

This happened approximately two years ago. Her husband is now president of the corporation. Recently, he wrote me a letter to say thanks for assisting his 'superb' wife. He says she has now become such an asset to him and his company that he insists she travel with him all over the world to meet clients and to look after them in her own special way.

2

How to be an executive, not consecutive, wife

It has been said that to be a 'good' corporate wife, you must be glamorous, poised, discreet, loyal and boundlessly ambitious, but only for your husband! Certainly in America many wives of high flyers thrive on being the partner of high-profile corporate or entrepreneurial men. Wives in the United Kingdom are now catching up . . . fast. Whereas business deals were often clinched between men only, wives are now required to entertain and woo potential and existing clients. Many women choose to become executive wives; many become consecutive wives.

An increasing number of executive marriages have foundered because a wife has not felt up to her new responsibilities. Although the breakup of a marriage comes as a personal blow, a divorce is no longer considered the kiss of death for an executive's career. The one who pays the price today is the first wife. Her fate is pronounced in those immortal words: *she didn't keep up.*

In this age of fast-moving, high-flying business, it is difficult for many wives – especially those devoted primarily to raising children – to catch up with their husbands' work. They quickly get out of touch and this obviously results in the gap between them and their husbands becoming much wider. Being a great housewife and mother appears to score less and less points in the career-oriented world of today. Women are beginning to question their role more and more each day. But as many executive wives are waking up to the challenges they must face, the executives they are married to are wanting to escape.

Other men find that their wives understand their situation and thrive on being on the corporate circuit. However, many of these are second wives. Second wives, it appears, make their husbands their Number One priority. They offer their executive husband pride of place. They possess a confidence and independence that eluded the first wives. As the second wife of a prominent executive said, there's no longer a prejudice against divorce in the corporate and political world. It's almost the opposite. In some instances, the man with the ageing, nice, matronly wife is frowned upon. He's seen as not keeping up appearances.

Successful men today simply 'expect' trophy wives more often than not. Self-indulgence becomes a final motivator for those who have succeeded professionally. They feel entitled to own the best – after all, they have earned it! The second wife – although beautiful, young, talented and probably successful on her own – is not the trophy that hangs on a wall like a moose head. She's dynamic in her own right.

But, of course, you can become a successful executive wife at any point in your life should you choose to do so. Since an executive's corporation is not a democracy that chooses an appropriate wife for its CEO by popular demand, the ability to carry on accordingly, discreetly and intelligently in partnership with your husband, rests with you.

The role of today's executive wife is not merely a ceremonial one. She must be able to tell what time it is in Bonn and know the exchange rate in Tokyo, feel comfortable in foreign cultures and mix well with corporate hierarchy, the community and the political scene. The new millenium beckons and most women who are married to men with power or public acclaim must re-tool their thinking to become the twenty-first century executive wife.

So, are you willing to give what it takes to become a successful corporate wife? If you have reacted strongly to anything I have said so far, that's great and this book is for you. Let us now go through some of what it does take to become an executive wife.

It requires quite a 'mix' of qualities. Many an active corporate wife, for instance, inspires a great deal of envy from housewives who do not get called upon to entertain. They see only the glamour of Bruce Oldfield and Yves Saint Laurent designer clothes, chauffeur-driven Rolls and Jaguars, stately homes, wonderful exotic holidays and so on. They don't know of the hours he spends away from home, of the many nights she spends alone. She is left to deal with the kids, sort out any domestic problems and, because her husband works up to fifteen hours per day, when he does come home, he is invariably exhausted.

But there are many attributes which a successful corporate wife has to possess. One of my first clients was the second wife of an executive of a very large and well-known international oil company. Let us call her Sally. She was glamorous, tall, with auburn hair and eyes of emerald green, well educated and certainly confident. I wondered why she had come to see me. After the second visit, I knew why.

She had been her husband's secretary for many years and had been a valauble addition to his business team. She knew almost as much about his business as he did. When his first wife died, it was natural for him to marry this woman who had 'held his hand' through many difficult as well as successful deals. His family liked and approved of Sally and accepted her, so all was seemingly well.

However, not everything was really well. She had a deep underlying fear that, having been his secretary, as his wife she would not now have such an active part to play. When in the office, she knew exactly what was going on. She talked and liaised with the main players in her husband's industry. She was informed. She knew what he had in mind when approaching a potentially large deal. Now, as his wife, she felt that his new secretary would know more than she did. Sally felt that her husband did not tell her as much simply because they saw less of one another than when they were working together. She felt left out. She was devastated.

This scenario has been played out by many people before Sally I am sure. Many wives will be able to understand this problem, and it is one with which I have to deal frequently throughout our seminars. It is the main theme which I stress however, to every woman who comes to see me. In order to be a successful corporate wife, you have to be informed . . . well informed! Whether you have worked with your husband or not, you should know about your husband's company, his

15

competitors, how the company was formed and by whom and you must obtain knowledge about future plans. Once in possession of this information, you have more control over any company situation you are faced with.

So, with Sally, we set about how to obtain such knowledge. Obviously, the main person for her to ask would be her husband. I suggested that she ask him to put aside at least one hour each week and always at the same time, so that it became a routine. This hour would be spent with the two of them discussing business details which would relate to Sally and the various functions which he wanted her to attend in the week ahead. I emphasised the fact that she should stress to him that she was still able to be his 'right hand woman'; that, if she was well-informed, she could use this knowledge to assist him in even greater capacity as his wife than when she was his secretary.

We discussed together exactly what she would say to him and suggested that, for the first few weeks at least, she should make a list of things to ask him so that she would not miss anything which might prove important later. In this way, a pattern would emerge whereby her husband also made a mental note to tell his wife at the allotted time each week and she would become not only well informed, but also a valuable asset to her very busy husband.

Some years later, I met Sally and her husband at a social event. She told me that her husband now would not make any major business decisions without first consulting her. She said that not only did she feel as if she 'belonged' but also felt that as his wife, she still contributed towards a very valuable business partnership.

In Sally's case, it was apparently quite simple to obtain the information she required, once she had set the initial pattern for her husband to confide in her. But what if your husband does not want to work in this way? Many husbands still want to see their wives as completely separate from their work. They don't want to discuss business affairs when they get home. They want to leave all that behind so that home is an oasis where business does not interfere. This is all very well, but equally, if they were questioned they would say, I am sure, that they also would want their wives to be seen by their colleagues and clients as informed, confident and able to cope when faced with corporate functions or entertaining.

In cases like these, wives have to take other courses of action. First of all, make a friend of your husband's secretary. She can so often tell you much of the information you need to know. If you are entertaining clients, for example, ask her to find out about their family, their likes and dislikes, so that you have some information to work on when you meet the clients. She might also be able to give you some idea why your husband is wishing to develop the business relationship, whether he is simply saying 'thank you' to them for being such good clients or whether he needs to develop the relationship still further in order to gain a large contract.

Sarah was a very young wife, mother of two small sons. Her husband was a high flyer in the advertising business. He was always out of the house by 6.30 am and never came home until late each evening. Because the babies were so young, he did all his corporate entertaining alone at large hotels or at exclusive clubs. Now, he had told her that he would like to bring a potentially large client and his wife home to dine with them. Apart from having to arrange and cook a suitable meal, she was left totally uninformed about the guests, because her husband had told her, 'I just want them to be here for a homely evening. Leave the business to me.' Her panic was very apparent.

Slowly, together we went through a procedure that made her feel totally confident in this, her first corporate assignment since the birth of the children. This event, she felt, was either to be the first of many such events or, if she made a mess of it, she equally felt she would not be asked again by her very ambitious husband, and she so wanted the former.

First of all, she telephoned her husband's secretary and got her to telephone the business associate's secretary to discover their culinary likes and dislikes. As the wife of the client was a vegetarian, this proved to be very important indeed. Secondly, together we telephoned the main Registrar of Companies. For a small sum, Sarah was able to receive a full print-out of the company in question and the names of their directors. From this information, she was able to see that the director who was coming to dinner had only recently been appointed. He had worked his way up from being general manager to a full-time director. The company was involved in skin-care products and from then until the date of the dinner, Sarah read as much as she could about it in women's magazines and the general press. She learned that they were now concentrating on new skin care which was not animal-tested. She assumed (and in this case, quite rightly) that the company, together with its new director, would be ready to launch a huge advertising campaign to stress the fact that no animals had been used to test their famous products.

Needless to say, the dinner was a success. Sarah was confident because she knew that her meal was enjoyed by all, especially the wife, who was very pleased to have a specially cooked vegetarian dish. She was confident she was able to talk efficiently and effectively to the potential client, who found he liked to discuss the merits of good skin care to someone who loved animals, but also wanted to keep her skin looking youthful. Their friendship began that evening and remains to this day.

Her husband, meanwhile, was thrilled with his wife and all that she had achieved for him on that evening, which was the first of many more.

3

How to gain confidence and exercise influence

'Just be yourself', I was so often told in my early days, when confidence was the pot of gold and I was at the other end of the rainbow. 'That's the last thing I want to be!', I thought to myself on the surface. But after thinking about it, I realised that 'just being myself' didn't work in an area where protocol prevailed. The well-intentioned people who offered me this advice did not experience a lack of confidence and self-esteem. If they did, they had a splendid way of concealing it.

Little did I know how accurate I was in that supposition. Everyone is searching at some time in their life for that something intangible they just can't get hold of. The unease you experience in what you perceive to be stressful circumstances is not foreign to others as well. In today's business climate, a sense of constant pressure invades all our lives. But certain people have learned to cope, to manage challenging situations better, while others wrongly feel they must surrender or battle alone.

Confidence and a sense of mastery are powerful weapons in successful interaction with other people. I've given up trying to understand confidence. It isn't important 'why' it works, it's only necessary to understand and firmly believe that it 'does' work. As a corporate wife, you need not feel intimidated when faced with your husband's colleagues, employees, constituents or whoever. They do not expect you to solve any global crises, but only wish to see you as a compassionate, considerate and respectful human being.

When I was very young, I thought that people at the top fully understood, and thus coped well with, everything that was happening . . . whether they were my parents, teachers, scientists, business leaders or prime ministers. I felt reassured knowing they had all the answers. But now that I am one of them – I touch them, see them, talk to them – I know better. Nothing could have been further from the truth! My confidence level certainly would have been higher if I had known then what I know now. I would have led a more adventurous instead of an intimidated life.

To become a successful executive wife does not mean that you will be put in some artificial mould; but, rather, you can develop a unique, discernible style that is unquestionably regarded as yours. Self-confidence is a power source. The more content you feel about yourself, the more you can rely on your natural energy and ability. Your mind works better, your thinking is more creative, your sense of intuition is more to the point. When you feel comfortable with yourself, regardless of the situation, you can handle successes and disappointments with greater equanimity. This protects you from negative, self-defeating behaviour. The more self-esteem you possess, the greater your confidence in your ability, the greater your enthusiasm for expanding your horizons.

Self-confidence is the foundation for declaring your ability in a way that allows you to use your skills most effectively. Nothing is more destructive to your ability to perform at peak level than constantly feeling uncertain about the role to which you are obliged to conform in the capacity of the executive wife. Certainly, our culture pays lip service to the ideal of individuality, but we all know how difficult it is to 'just be ourselves' when a specific result is often expected during a business social function. Hence, the greater your self-confidence, the more alert and alive each opportunity becomes, and the more frequently you can reach high levels of success.

William James, the American psychologist, once wrote that most of us live 'in a very restricted circle of our potential being'. We seem to ignore our strong qualities and live up to our weaknesses instead. The instinct to do very little, to remain put, to choose security over challenge, to be a follower instead of a leader, and to accept second-best is too often more powerful than the will to get the most out of life. If you find that you regularly tolerate feelings of disappointment, have problems in dealing with your husband's colleagues, and suffer regrets about how you could have handled various encounters because you don't feel empowered to do something concrete about it, then you have a lack of self-confidence. 'People don't lack strength,' wrote Victor Hugo, 'they lack will'. You don't *have* to use only a minor portion of your potential ability and intelligence. Why experience only a fraction of the satisfaction and success you are entitled to? If we utilise less than ten per cent of our intellectual and emotional capacity, we possess a tremendous reserve of ability that goes unused. By tapping into your reserves for greater self-esteem and self-confidence, you become closer to achieving your goals on a daily basis. The greater your self-confidence, the more energy, enthusiasm, creativity, and courage you'll have at your disposal to create the life you truly want. Increasing your self-confidence opens new dimensions of professional ability and constantly increases your daily enjoyment of new conquests, greater challenges. You graduate from a certain level of functioning where will, self-confidence and energy are low to a greater level where these qualities are abundant.

I find that too many wives who come to see me routinely tend to underestimate themselves. They sell short their ability and shy away from the challenges that promote the growth of self-discovery and adventure. That is the way to view the corporate or political structure: it's not something odd and foreign, or dull and uninspiring, but something adventurous and challenging. It doesn't take long for these women to discover that their capacity for self-confidence is always far, far greater than they give themselves credit for. Only by accepting the challenges that face them, can they tap their full store of energy, intelligence, vitality and all the satisfaction that goes with becoming adequately involved in their husband's careers.

Such a challenge was accepted, however reluctantly, by a client named Maggie. On most occasions, wives find out about my executive courses from the press or by recommendations from other wives who have gone through the programme. Sometimes, however, it is the husband who will contact us. They genuinely want their wives to become more involved in their affairs, or they desperately want them to enjoy more fully the role of being a corporate wife.

Maggie was one of the latter. Her husband's secretary telephoned me and eventually had to make three separate appointments, as each of the others were cancelled at the very last moment because Maggie could not face attending. Eventually, she did come to one of our classes but with her husband's secretary in tow.

Maggie was very attractive, exceptionally groomed but extremely timid. She met her husband as a teenager and they married shortly thereafter. Maggie stayed at home from the beginning of their marriage and soon began a family. Her husband was the works manager of a large industrial company but possessed an extremely ambitious streak. Indeed, he worked hard at his position and eventually moved to a leading company as its managing director. He became increasingly keen for Maggie to become much more involved in the entertaining of potential clients and to be seen with him whenever a corporate event was taking place. Maggie, meanwhile, was absolutely terrified at the very thought of this and simply wanted to remain at home with her two daughters, now teenagers. I later learned from her that she had felt totally inadequate and also had an underlying fear that because her husband had moved on so quickly, he would not want her any more (a common trend among corporate wives with high-flyer husbands). Maggie was a challenge in more ways than one.

One of the first things we ask our wives to do at a session is to be interviewed in front of a television camera. It is one thing which I think most people do not like to do, because they feel uneasy about it. I can certainly understand why. To be questioned in front of a camera can be very daunting but, again, most of our wives are thrilled once they have done it and subsequently see the video. We ask them questions about themselves and their families and also about current world affairs. It gives us an immediate idea of what our clients know, how they react to certain questions and how they cope when they obviously don't know the answers. This assessment can later be effectively used to assist the wives to overcome their individual problems much more easily. Very often they can identify certain habits or mannerisms, once they examine themselves on video.

One of the questions we always ask is, 'How do you get on with your neighbours?' Maggie simply replied that she lived in a house surrounded by seventy acres of land and she really did not know if she had any neighbours! The only people she saw throughout the day were her children and/or her husband, plus some shop assistants when she went shopping in the nearby town, which was some fifteen miles away. Can you imagine how lonely and isolated this poor woman felt, sitting in her newly acquired huge home with only herself to talk to? It's no wonder she was lonely, frightened and lacked confidence. She was most afraid, we learned much later, of losing her husband, because she just did not want to take part in any corporate activity. She felt she was not good enough to be seen as her husband's partner in front of his business colleagues and clients. Consequently, her husband continued to entertain alone and away from home, which caused Maggie to feel alienated to an even greater degree. It became a vicious circle.

Strangely, however, Maggie coped much better than most with the video interview, but obviously she desperately needed to have confidence instilled into her, to make her realise that she was a worthwhile person in her own right. The challenge was for Maggie to feel good about herself once more. Together we discussed various ways of doing this, and I suggested she came to see me alone without her husband's secretary and without the other wives. She would not agree to come without the secretary, but was happy to come without the other wives and have some 'one-to-one' guidance.

First, I started a series of programmes on how she could cope at various corporate functions commencing with the simple cocktail reception, for example, at her husband's office. By introducing role play where she could practise 'small talk', bit by bit she learnt how to be more in control of conversations. She learnt that she should always introduce herself quite confidently even if she did not feel it and always with a smile (many people do not smile, especially when they are nervous) and to offer a firm, confident handshake. Simply by doing these few initial movements she discovered already she was feeling a little more happy – she had something to think about which stopped her from just standing there wondering if people would like her.

Secondly, I told her to remember to introduce various questions regarding a fellow guest's wellbeing. Remembering that people like to talk about themselves, I gradually made her believe that asking about their interests, for example, would lead into a conversation. Using these techniques, she could ask about work, family and even current issues of the day – anything to get the other person talking! She appeared to learn easily and certainly did very well in her role playing. But then came the first test.

Her husband was arranging a small reception for a long-term employee who was retiring from the company. As managing director, he invited a selected number of colleagues and the retiring man's wife, plus some of his immediate professional friends. In many ways, this was one of the most difficult functions to attend as even hardened businessmen find this type of environment difficult. However, Maggie was determined to attend. Armed with lots of possible questions to ask, having first rehearsed them with us over and over again, she duly set off. We did not forget about her wardrobe either. She selected exactly the outfit that not only looked correct for the occasion, but also felt right for her. Nothing could go wrong . . .

Her telephone call came as I was arriving at the office. Maggie was in tears. Unfortunately, on arrival, she discovered that her husband's colleagues had also brought their wives and this was not expected. Maggie had been previously told by her husband that she was to be the only executive wife in attendance for this occasion. This was very important to her since she felt she could 'practise' her newly-found skills on people without the other wives for competition, so as not to feel threatened. This insecurity was emphasised in particular by one of the wives who was always in the 'front line' on this particular occasion, and who apparently made it very evident that Maggie behaved like a mouse. Added to this, Maggie's husband was not well and could not assist her in any way. The evening, in Maggie's eyes, was a disaster. Any confidence which she may have acquired had completely vanished. All she wanted to do was to go back home and do her crocheting. Maggie crocheted for hours at a time, designing and making beautiful table mats, baby clothes and exquisite bedcovers.

However, with a little encouragement from both her husband and myself, she decided to give us another try. Once again we went through the questions and answers method, how to dress confidently, listening, and how to keep up with current issues in order to have many items to discuss. To be fair to Maggie, she also made herself attend many other functions – dinners, receptions, corporate entertaining events and luncheons – but seemingly all to no avail. She was stll finding it difficult to cope and I was equally determined that she would! Here was a woman who really had so much to give! I knew that once she could regain some confidence she would stop shutting the rest of the world away and enjoy life to the full.

You can imagine therefore the joy I felt when after a number of months' training, I received an elated telephone call from Maggie. I knew that she had attended an institution dinner with her husand the previous evening and we had gone through the techniques with her again. The evening began badly, she says, as most of the guests she was introduced to were very much older and were all in business, even the women. Halfway through the evening however, she met a lady who, when Maggie asked what her interests were, answered that it was crochet! Picture her absolute delight when she knew that she had found someone to whom she could talk about her own interests with ease. They apparently spent the rest of the evening discussing various designs and colours. Suddenly, she said, all the things we had discussed with her and trained her for came into focus. Maggie and Eve, her newfound friend, recently set up a company together through which their combined skills and designs are now sold worldwide.

From the moment Maggie realised that there was something she could do, and could contribute to the world in her own way, her confidence grew in leaps and bounds. Finding something she knew she could do well, and felt in control of, changed her life significantly. Maggie could now enjoy all aspects of her life, not least that of being a corporate wife.

Confidence breeds confidence and we all have to work at making it happen, even if some of us do not always feel as confident in some situations as we would like. But appearing confident makes people respond to us in a positive and enjoyable manner. Needless to say, I have the most beautiful set of crochet table mats which I bring out at special dinner parties and I always think of Maggie when I do so. They were her first gift to me as a very confident person indeed!

Confidence can work as such a powerful prime motivator in

your life, too. When you think of yourself as significant, as being able to stand out in your own right, as someone who is willing and capable to follow things through, you think of yourself as a successful person, which is far greater than any other attribute you may possess. Why, the satisfaction of being an achiever, of being recognised as one who can 'do it' is enough to boost anyone's self-esteem and to promote that powerful feeling of self-worth. Once you cross that fascinating bridge of wondering whether you can achieve something seemingly difficult, you arrive at a splendid state of infinite possibilities. When you're up against the south-west face of Mount Everest, you explore the intriguing possibiliies of how it can be climbed; you no longer shy away. Such is the case with confidence.

I learned this first-hand at the beginning of my career when I first decided to start my own company. I had contacted a number of major UK companies offering my public relations services and was therefore delighted to receive a telephone call from one large international construction and property company. After seeing my presentation, they eventually gave me the job of looking after their company for a trial period of six months. (I am happy to say that the company is still one of my clients, even after all these years.)

The first assignment I received from them was to arrange a management conference in Cyprus. The management teams from all the international branches of the company were to assemble on this lovely island and I chose a beautiful hotel ten miles from Limassol, set in magnificent countryside with a private beach. I was extremely nervous, as this was my first assignment.

As I said goodbye to my husband at the airport, I felt physically sick. What on earth was I doing? How could I possibly think this would be successful? As I arrived in Cyprus one day prior to the teams' arrival, I could not appreciate the wonderful scenery or enjoy the friendly islanders. All I could think about was how on earth was I going to cope. Thirty men were arriving the next day. I had to do my utmost to make the whole week enjoyable for them as well as to ensure all the working elements of the conference ran smoothly. However, nothing had prepared me for the arrival at Cyprus airport of thirty very drunk individuals. Apparently they had drunk the plane dry of

champagne and they were on a high, over-reacting to everything, all trying to outdo one another. I had completely forgotten how men act when they are gathered together and away
from home!

The first evening went reasonably well, in spite of this, and I
eventually retired to bed. The next morning, as I was checking
the lecture suites, audio-visual equipment and the like, it came
to my attention that some of the delegates had stayed up all
night drinking and had thrown a colleague into the swimming
pool. This was obviously due to very high spirits but was nevertheless frowned upon by the hotel management. I was certainly
not confident enough to discuss this with the chairman and just
hoped this sort of thing would not be the norm throughout the
week. Later that day, I was told by one of the quieter executives
that the men in question were based in Saudi Arabia. As you
know, alcohol is banned in that country, so when the opportunity presented itself for them to enjoy a drink, they went
overboard. They were top-level executives and they behaved
professionally in every other way, but were also determined to
work and play hard during their visit to Cyprus.

The next morning I was called into the manager's office. Three
of the same executives had again stayed up all night and had
disrupted the swimming pool. What was I going to do about it? I
decided the only way was to approach the chairman directly and
ask him to have a talk with his delegates. He agreed and spoke to
them all at the first lecture of the day. However, that evening I
decided to make myself stay awake late enough to go down to
the bar and check if all was well. So at 2 am I duly went on the
prowl. I was very nervous. If some of the delegates were there,
how would they react to me? (Yes, of course they were usually
well behaved and well-mannered, but people change when they
are full of alcohol.)

When I got to the bar, it was empty and I was just about to dive
back to my room when I heard a loud crash coming from the
central lobby. When I got there, I was met by the sight of four
'troubleshooters' who were sprawled across the lobby settees,
bottles all around them and generally causing havoc with the
hotel porters. I was shaking with nervousness, but suddenly
found myself saying in an authoritative voice that they should
clean up and check out! I told them how disgusted I was and that

I would personally ensure that they were thrown out of the hotel unless they vowed to change their ways.

Remember, this was my very first assignment, I had everything to lose if I did not handle things well. I certainly was not confident, but I knew I had to look and act as though I was in charge. Up until that evening, most of the delegates had hardly noticed or indicated that I was there at all, but I noticed that on this particular evening, they responded instantly by leaving the lobby! I am sure this was because they felt instinctively that I had every right to carry out my threat and this would cause embarrassment all round. The next day, again feeling very apprehensive, I went to the conference suite to prepare for the main lecture. As each of the delegates in question came into the suite, as though it had been pre-arranged among themselves, one by one they apologised and assured me there would not be a recurrence of the previous night's activities.

From then on, I felt that I had earned the respect of the delegates and my confidence grew. By initially acting as though I had all the confidence in the world, I suddenly did! We went on to enjoy the rest of the conference without incident and I still arrange their annual conferences in many other countries. I realised that the executives, like so many others, were all very hard-working and under a great deal of pressure to maintain profits in a very competitive marketplace, and they simply had to let off steam sometimes. However, they never did so in front of me again.

That event taught me a very valuable lesson. To act confidently makes you feel confident, a feeling which grows constantly but nevertheless needs to be reinforced from time to time. This was emphasised still further when the same international company asked me to look after the president of Mexico, who was coming to London on a private visit. As the company's guest, he and his entourage were to take part in a series of high-level business meetings. My company was delegated to arrange the week's activities, which resulted in a combination of business meetings, political meetings and receptions/dinners, etc. It presented a very busy schedule.

All went very well until the fourth day of the visit. I had taken the whole floor of the prestigious Hyde Park Hotel in Knightsbridge. We had been involved in a series of meetings throughout the morning followed by a luncheon at the House of Lords. We returned to the hotel to have a few hours welcome break before preparing for a dinner with leading industrialists. My hotel room, like all the others, faced the beautiful Hyde Park – that wonderful oasis of green lawns and immaculate flower beds in the centre of London. I remember looking out over the park and as I watched I saw coming towards me and the hotel the Royal Horse Guards parading as usual on their beautiful black horses. I felt very proud as I watched them pass, the guards wearing their steel breast-plates and helmets with the distinctive plumage. As they passed by my window, I returned to my room and the rest of the day's duties.

It was at that precise moment that the whole building completely shook to its very foundations. Ornaments, furniture, pictures, all fell to the floor. All the windows were smashed and I was thrown to the ground. I could not believe what was happening. I crawled to the balcony via the smashed glass. What I saw was something I will never forget: a bomb had gone off right in the middle of the parade. There were bodies and horses lying everywhere, complete carnage. People were screaming, running around, not knowing what to do. I was absolutely stunned and seemed unable to do anything but stand in paralysed stupidity and watch the terrible sight in front of me. I learned afterwards that it was an IRA bomb, one of three which were exploded throughout London on that day causing havoc and many deaths.

Once I came to my senses, my first concern was to establish whether the president was alive and well. I somehow felt personally responsible for his safety. However, it soon became clear that all was well and, like me and most of the hotel guests, we were only very shaken and not hurt. My next horrified reaction, however, came the following day. I was scheduled to take the president and his colleagues to visit Ireland for the weekend. Should we still make the visit? The chairman of the client company met me and explained that in spite of everything that had happened, the president still wanted to go to Ireland and that he also would like to continue with our plans. Would I have the confidence to proceed? Although we had security guards attached to the entourage, the responsibility would be mainly mine as there would be no personnel from the international client company. I would be accompanying them alone. I thought about it a great deal but eventually decided that we would go ahead with the plans. After all, I reasoned, the IRA were not after the Mexicans, so all should be well.

I arrived at our hotel in Dublin and soon began to think differently! As usual, I arrived before my clients to ensure all was well with the accommodation. But on talking to the hotel management, I discovered that nothing much had been prepared and I was met with a complete air of indifference. I was mortified, and even more so when I returned to my room to find a note had been pushed underneath the door. It said 'Britisher, go home!' The Irish are among the most friendly and hospitable people in the world, but there is a small element who do not like the British and I had found a hotel with one of them. From that moment on, I had to quadruple check everything and continually look over my shoulder. I did not for one moment think that anything serious would happen to me, only that my mission would be made difficult. Added to this worry, the president and his colleagues did not seem to be enjoying the visit. We travelled around Ireland and saw many of the beautiful spots that this wonderful country has to offer. We visited an Irish party where true Irish spirit was shown as well as drunk, but throughout the whole time, they were extremely polite but certainly not enthusiastic. I was devastated. What a weekend! My confidence was ebbing.

Late on Sunday afternoon, we returned from visiting a typical Irish country club. We had two or three hours before dinner and our return to England was to be early the following morning. The president requested that we join him in his suite for drinks, where we sat around discussing our visit. I was immediately made aware that everyone seemed to be more relaxed. Certainly, the president was smiling and made jokes with everyone. It was only when we sat down to dinner in the main restaurant of the hotel that his aide said to me that the president had been very worried for me during our visit and had ensured that one of his security men was protecting me, as well as him, throughout the weekend. The dinner was tremendously successful, with everyone enjoying the marvellous Irish food. So good and so much of it – would anything be left for the Irish, I wondered?

However, you can imagine my concern and embarrassment

when suddenly the president stood up and started to sing! – not a happy 'jingle' but rather like the old, Mario Lanza-type, dramatic song, and in a roaring baritone voice. The other hotel guests stared in amazement, especially when he finished and then invited his colleagues, one by one, to sing individually to us. His aide said this was the true Mexican way of saying how much they had enjoyed the meal. I spoke quickly to the restaurant manager about this and he, of course, let it continue because it was totally unlike a drunken brawl but something rather beautiful, particularly as they all seemed to have excellent voices. The evening finished with many other hotel guests joining us from the restaurant. A pianist arrived. Everyone sang along. This was truly an international evening where music had brought us all together, overcoming all difficulties. It was indeed a memorable visit and quite an unconventional evening.

Looking back, I am glad I did not lose my confidence when it mattered most. I would not have missed that occasion for anything! The significance of such an opportunity is that it specifically focused my thoughts on action. Having such a focus is a necessary part of success. Instead of wandering aimlessly, you have a specific job to do, a purpose and a goal which result in a documented achievement. What may appear as an overwhelming vista of chaos is scaled down to the particular goal. As you achieve each such goal, so much less will your world appear threatening. By facing the challenges that confront you, you change the course of destiny, you take control of your situations instead of allowing situations to take control of you.

This could not be more true than in the case of the Princess of Wales. We all remember seeing the shy, blushing girl as she walked down the aisle on the arm of Prince Charles. No doubt, even then, there were many advisers offering their services to the Princess in order to assist her in successfully achieving the role of what must be the ultimate executive wife. But I feel sure that even they could not prepare her for the daunting task of being a stateswoman, a mother and a wife, constantly in the public eye. Over the years, we have seen her emerge from just being seen at her husband's side on public occasions and blushing painfully every time anyone spoke to her, to becoming a confident, independent person in her own right.

But we are well aware that she, too, has had to work at

achieving this, and work very hard indeed. Apart from the grooming and lessons in protocol, she achieves and maintains excellent health with the aid of good diet and lots of exercise. She proudly displays a good figure which enhances her new confident image. In addition to this, she has researched where best to expand her own talents to suit her role as the next Queen of England. Her work with children, Aids patients, the deaf, and former drug addicts, is a direct result of that eagerness to fulfil her role.

Because the Princess has now made herself better informed, she is able to make speeches which have made a significant impact on the people who matter. She has become very much a person in her own right and, needless to say, this has made her look and feel more and more confident. She has succeeded in her role of being the wife of a very important person, but because she has exceeded all expectations, she is now in great demand with or without her husband. When it matters most, she is equally seen as the other person in a very successful partnership.

Gaining confidence need not always be about the 'big' things in life. Small things, which too many of us would find totally irrelevant, are to others the reasons they do not enjoy life to the full.

A very sweet girl who attended our classes seemed to be rather bored with our activities. After a while, I asked her, during a break, if she was enjoying it or was there something specific she wished to find out. She said there was, but she felt silly asking me about it. We agreed to meet privately after everyone had gone home. She was just nineteen and had become engaged to a young man who came from a very well known, aristocratic family. Her fiancé was the heir to the family fortune and the family had accepted her. The plans for the wedding were under way. What, then, was the problem? Eventually, she 'confessed' that although her fiancé's brothers seemed to like her, one of them had made a derogatory remark about her table manners. She was extremely upset about this. She told me that it made a difference to her relationship with her fiancé, as he did not defend her and she felt undermined. She was a 'well brought up young lady', as my mother would say, and had been to one of the best private schools for girls in the country.

So she had been taught how to cope at large formal dinner parties – to start using the cutlery from the outside in, for example. Her future brother-in-law had made his remark, however, when she was helping herself to the fruit. Apparently, it was simply an unfortunate remark which, consequently, made her lose all confidence in front of him and the rest of the family. Each meal with them subsequently, formal or otherwise, became a nightmare and gradually she began to wonder if she was the right person after all for her fiancé to marry.

Once we let our minds take over in this way, we begin to lose confidence in every way. Once our confidence is boosted, it grows and grows. Unfortunately, the reverse can happen if we allow our minds to extend to the negative possibilities. Well, I am sure, you are already ahead of me as to what we did to help this poor girl. I simply arranged for her to eat a whole lot of fruit with us and go through each and every fruit in turn.

My friend Moyra Bremner, who has written the marvellous etiquette book *Enquire Within Upon Everything!*, writes: 'If a table is laid with a fruit knife and fork you don't touch the fruit with your hands at all except to help yourself. Instead, you use them to cut the fruit into quarters and peel it. Then cut off small slices and eat them on the fork. If there is only a fruit knife, cut the fruit in question in quarters, peel it, cut off a small section at a time and eat it in your fingers. Small fruit, such as cherries or plums, are simply eaten in the fingers'.

I gave Anne a copy of her book for reference and we duly went through the motions with all the fruit we had, until we came to the dreaded *grapes*. She simply froze when I suggested she take some. Gradually, I persuaded her to eat them, separating them from the main stem with her fingers and popping them into her mouth. It was then that she told me that *this* was the fruit about which she had been reprimanded by her future brother-in-law. She was determined that she should *peel* each grape before eating it. We then began what can only be described as one of the oddest experiences I have ever had. We were each taking grapes and gently peeling them with our fingers and knife before putting them into our mouths. She was determined to do it right, and of course eventually she succeeded. For one week, every day she came to the office with bunches of grapes. It was a marvellous diet!

This meant so much to her that after a time she began to calm down and feel confident enough to face her husband's brother. I also suggested she attend a few confidence lessons, and after a short while she became the happy and confident person she should have always been when just about to marry the one she loved. As a postscript, I told her that if ever her confidence failed her again on this issue, she could always refuse the fruit course!

4

How to use knowledge to gain power

This is an age in which the mind is monarch. People have long known that knowledge is power. This universal fact is reinforced every day of our lives. In today's world, intelligence is an extraordinarily bankable commodity. High status is bestowed upon the well informed. Broad and specific knowledge guarantees an unquestionable and unmistakable eminence. 'She knows what she is talking about' is a response that everyone considers to be very high praise indeed. On the contrary, shallow glibness merits only suspicion and rejection. 'A blabbermouth' is one of the most hideous forms of insult.

Among your friends and peers are doubtless those who cautiously offer their opinions. If they are not supported by genuine evidence, they tend to withhold comment. Such people are usually trusted and respected. Their judgement is valued. But a portion of those you know may frequently 'run off at the mouth' every chance they get. This is particularly disturbing when they have little or no idea of what they are talking about. You may absolutely adore them in every other way, but when they have an opinion to express, you turn a blind eye.

'I could excuse being defeated but never being surprised,' said Frederick the Great. These are words we should all live by. You certainly cannot be in control of any situation to a reasonable degree today unless you possess top-rate information. Surprisingly enough, the information you need to be armed with as the excecutive or political wife is not difficult to obtain. In fact, it can be rather simple and not terribly time-consuming if you know what to look for, whom to ask for assistance and where to find it.

Let us now take one situation where many executive wives find themselves on numerous occasions. Your husband wishes you to accompany him to meet a man and his wife for a meal. The man is a potential client of your husband's company. They have had the usual business presentations and meetings, plus negotiations, which have all gone well. The man has invited you and your husband to meet his wife and to dine at his London club. You have been told by your husband that this particular evening could make or mar his company's future. You are faced with what could be seen as a terrifying prospect! You are aware that your contribution to this event is crucial. You must do and say everything right!

All you can establish from your husband, who is chairman of an advertising company, is that the man, Joe, is the president of a major computer company. His account would mean huge revenue for a contract lasting at least three years. Taking the most positive action, you realise that to have confidence, you must be informed. To be informed is to do your homework before the evening begins! So let's begin by finding out as much about the computer company as possible.

By telephoning the Companies Registration Office in London, you can establish precisely when and where the company was formed. Upon request, you can have a print-out sent to you showing the date of formation and the names of the directors. From this information, you can establish, for example, that this particular computer company was formed in 1984 and is a UK subsidiary of an American computer corporation. It is a completely separate company, however, but has the umbrella of the American corporation to give a corporate identity, logo, literature, etc., and you learn later that this corporate identity has to be maintained by all subsidiaries worldwide.

By now you have got your husband's secretary on your side and by asking her to give you the registration number of the computer company (which by law has to be printed at the bottom of all company stationery), you can again contact the Companies Registration Office. This time, you can request a print-out of all the company accounts up to the last twelve months. All limited companies have to show their accounts each year in this way, so that anyone who wishes can have access to these simply by identifying the registration number. Alternatively, by telephoning the company direct, you may well be sent last year's financial report. Many major companies employ specialised public relations experts to produce these annual financial reports, especially when they have success stories to tell.

Whichever way you choose to find out this information, you will by now have established that their profits have leaped with each year's trading. You will discover that this particular company has gone from being a very insignificant subsidiary to become a major force within the UK. You will also note that it has now begun to buy out other large computer companies and has become a large personal computer manufacturer with only one other major competitor in Britain. By now you have established that this company, in the few years since it began trading in the UK, has become one of the major computer companies in the country. You have also established what the president looks like and you know some of his directors by name.

It is useful to note that the same procedure can provide the same results if, for example, the company in question deals in any other products or services. As long as you find the registration number, you will have access to the financial accounts, as previously mentioned. Trade magazines are available for almost any group or trade. In England alone there are over fifteen thousand different trade magazines printed as well as other international magazines which promote other countries' products and services.

However, to get back to our situation . . . Having looked through all the computer magazines to find out as much as you can about the company, you may well wish to look also at the more prestigious magazines, such as *Business Magazine*, *International Management*, or *Management Today*. These publications give a more general outlook on certain companies and very often do profile articles on the company and how it has succeeded over the years. This would give you much more background information. (Alternatively, when I want to find this type of more detailed information, I telephone the company's press office and ask to have copies of recent general articles. They are always happy to send these and I have found most press personnel very helpful.) Regarding Joe's company, you find that there was a company feature written recently which tells many more details about the man himself! – Marvellous!

Armed with all this knowledge, you are already beginning to feel more confident about knowing some of the background of the president's company. But you have only just begun. . . !

Your next task is to buy all the computer magazines you can see. You are suddenly made aware that there are articles everywhere about this company, their new products, their service, how they have improved their computers to fit every need, and to suit every profession. You learn that they have recently developed the most convenient lap-top computer ever invented. (This means that business people everywhere are able to fit a computer into their briefcases and use them, literally on their laps, when travelling in a train, plane and even in a car – when someone else is driving!) The feature on the new product has a photograph of Joe, the UK president, showing how small the computer is, so you can see exactly what he looks like – a man of about forty years of age, tall, dark and, yes, reasonably handsome.

For the weeks prior to the evening, you will buy the *Financial Times* and check each day the value of the company's shares. You will be able to monitor that even over the last couple of weeks their shares have gone up over 15p per share. Things are obviously very good! If more information is required on this particular aspect, you would read the *Herald Tribune* or the *New York Times* to establish how the American side is doing. In studying these international newspapers, you may find other articles written on the success of the American corporation in general.

This has proved enormously helpful to you, because you read that he has a wife and two children and that he previously was managing director of the NFU and responsible for over twenty thousand employees. He came from a farming family but did not enjoy farming, much to his father's displeasure. Imagine the scoop you have here! If the situation presents itself to you during the evening, you could talk about family relations, for example, or why he did not like farming. What made him go into 'modern' technology and does he now enjoy his comparatively new role?

At this point, and with the information already established, you need not proceed further. You have enough to get you through the evening and can find out more if required, through direct conversation with Joe and his wife. However, it is very useful, too, to keep up with current and international events so that you are able to converse in perhaps more general terms.

You will therefore ensure that you read all the national newspapers each day. Simply by reading the most prominent headlines plus the first two paragraphs of an article, you can quickly discover what is being reported. This quick method of reading ensures that you do not have to take hours going through all the written material available but, at the same time, ensures that you are very well informed. Another idea for keeping up with current events is to catch the daily news programmes on television or radio. Either can be switched on and giving you the information you need, when you are doing other things like getting the breakfast, doing the ironing or cooking. This constant reminder from the media assists you mentally to retain what is happening in the world today.

You may find, however, that you want to have more knowledge of Joe and his immediate family. This would prove useful to talk about to his wife, perhaps, and to compare your family with hers. Again, I always find the secretaries very helpful in this instance. By telephoning his secretary and explaining exactly what you want to know about Joe and his family and why, I am sure you will find her extremely helpful. She will tell you that he has a boy and girl, both teenagers. The boy is at university reading languages whilst the girl is at ballet school, as she wishes to become a prima ballerina! All this information you can tuck away into your mind and use whenever you wish and because of this background knowledge, your confidence soars. All you need now is to convince your husband that you definitely need a new outfit!

On this occasion, the dinner is to be held at Joe's exclusive London club. Just prior to the evening, it is useful to telephone the club itself simply to find out about it. Where is the bar situated, for example? How many members has it? What is required to become a member? The staff are always eager to help, I find, especially if you say you are thinking of becoming a member yourself. This information will again assist you in gaining increasing confidence. You are then not in awe of certain situations within the club, you know the form, you know what is expected of you. There is nothing worse than appearing at such a club in casual attire when formality is required at all times. Most prestigious clubs do not allow men in without wearing ties, and you need to know all such information beforehand. Some twenty-four hours before the evening itself, it is useful to go quietly through all you know about Joe and his company. Look again through all the literature you have gathered and the notes you have made on his company. Put on the outfit you are going to wear for the evening. Get all your accessories right and leave them in a safe place so that you can find them easily. Put a spare pair of tights or stockings near to hand or even to take with you in case of emergencies.

Whenever I have an important occasion such as this, I also go through a routine which might be helpful to you. I imagine the evening, the people involved in it. I already know what Joe looks like; I can imagine him talking with me. I also go through some of the questions he might ask and speak the answers out loud. This somehow confirms what is likely to happen and I already know what my response is going to be. This routine builds up the confidence you have already acquired and by going through many of the conversations you are likely to have, when the time comes for them, you are already practised enough to cope with any of the answers. By speaking the words out loud, you find that you can convey supreme confidence at all times. When eventually the evening begins, armed with all your previous knowledge of Joe, his family, his club and his company, you know that you have plenty to talk about, you have as much knowledge and probably more, than your husband. You are able to play your role superbly.

Let us now assume that the evening has taken place. You have done extremely well. Both Joe and his wife Liz seemed to enjoy your conversations and, more importantly, your company. You have been congratulated by your husband for exceeding his expectations and you hear from him that he has now obtained Joe's very significant account for his company. Both your husband and you know that you have played a very powerful part in achieving this account. However, this means that you must carry on the good work. You will therefore be meeting Joe and

Liz frequently at social occasions when your husband's company entertains. Therefore it is essential that you monitor the success of your husband's company towards that of Joe's, and at the same time keep up with events happening within Joe's business. The most obvious tactic to employ is, of course, to ask your own husband initially what is happening with this account. Is it as large as he first thought? Is he finding that the computer industry is very competitive? If so, is Joe's company, with the help of your husband's talents, keeping above the main competition? By finding out the answers to these and other questions, you will be able to keep in touch with current events. If he gives you these answers frequently, then all is well and good, but the chances are that he is already busy with another potential customer and cannot and does not give his time to you and your queries. So you must obtain these facts for yourself.

The first thing you must ensure is that all the facts you have already acquired, together with the computer literature, are placed away in a file for future reference when required. By now, you will have added other details which you have found out at your meeting with Joe and his wife. You may have discovered that they are mainly vegetarians, that his wife is interested in ethnic arts, or that they both like tennis. All these details will be included in your own personal filing system so that you can refer to these when required and add to them when other information is obtained.

Each week you should make an effort to buy some of the more prominent computer magazines. In this way, you can discover the new services and new activities that Joe's company is currently involved in. Similarly, it is good advice to keep a check on the current share market prices so that you can find out immediately if these go down and explore why they have done so, or else establish why they have gone up and why the City appears to look upon the company favourably. Ask to be put on the mailing list of the company's press office so that you will be notified of any movement the computer company is involved in. Generally, be open to receive any news from any part of the media regarding this company. By doing so well at your initial evening meeting, this must be maintained throughout any future meetings with both Joe and/or his wife. When next you are going to meet them, you should again look through your notes and information on more personal issues, so that you can continue with your interest and succeed with the business relationship.

It is equally essential to monitor your husband's company and how it is proceeding with the account. Again, seek the assistance of your husband's secretary and ask her to tell you what she knows. Get copies of the company's accounts and see how Joe's account is affecting the overall revenue of the business. If you get on well with his other directors, you may well be able to ask their advice as to how the account is proceeding. Once you are known for your enthusiasm for helping in every way possible within your husband's company, you will be treated with great respect and you will find that your husband's colleagues will be only too pleased to provide you with the details you require. However, your approaches to them must be done in a diplomatic way, so you are not seen as a 'busybody'. Once you achieve this, you will discover your husband and his colleagues will want you to be involved with other new clients as well as with existing ones. They will admire your professionalism in achieving your own goals in order to obtain and maintain a client. Your techniques will prove to them that they really can become an integral part of the business activity.

It will also lead you to feel more and more confident. Knowing that you can do, and be seen to be doing, something extra towards obtaining new clients, will enable you to have much more in-depth conversations with your husband's colleagues at corporate functions. Instead of wondering what you are going to say, you have already achieved a sound business relationship with them. You immediately are involved, perhaps much more than any other wife, which ultimately makes you feel needed and in control.

You might like to know of a young executive wife who recently told me of a successful ritual she developed when it came to information gathering. Her husband is an investment banker with a very well-established firm, whose time is divided between the London and New York branches. Victoria often accompanies him and has even established residences in both cities. She loves to stroll down Fifth Avenue to the Plaza Hotel on windy and golden autumn afternoons. The rush of the crowds and the vitality of Manhattan gives her a certain welcome energy. But in order not to make the time appear fruitless, she will visit a favourite bookshop across the street from Trump Tower and browse through new or unfamiliar sections. Her favourite publication is a weekly magazine called *World Press Review*. She's thrilled with it, because it saves her a great deal of time. It provides a unique collection of articles on current events as they appeared in most major newspapers and periodicals worldwide. Conservative, moderate and liberal press is equally represented, as articles are reprinted in English. This provides her with an unbiased and selective source of global information. There are also news briefs and cartoons on all important issues of the day.

Victoria also makes a habit of stopping by the business section and browsing over titles that might deal with a current issue that's in the news, which she will tuck away for in-flight reading. One evening, she told her husband what the Japanese thought about the failure of a leading American brokerage house and how the Russians interpreted Black Monday. Clearly, her husband thought she had been working very hard in keeping up. However, the next day Victoria spend the afternoon in the lavish stores of New York and not behind the pages of the *Financial Times*!

Victoria always made the process of being informed a pleasure. At home, she created a cosy area for morning reading. On the 22nd floor of her Manhattan apartment, she transformed a brilliantly sun-filled room that provides a glorious view of the New York skyline into her own personal space. She laid a sage and apricot rug over a basket-weave motif parquet floor that provided a sober foundation underfoot. She filled the small room with green plants and crystal bowls with aromatic potpourri. The bookshelves on one side of the wall contained such a variety of titles that no one could truly establish the occupant's identity by merely browsing through them. Spread across the table was her staple morning reading: the *New York Times*, the *Wall Street Journal*, the *Times* of London and even a couple of tabloid dailies whose titles she won't reveal!

After Victoria's husband heads for the office, she does not spend more than an hour looking at the news of the day. If there is a particular article of interest, she saves it for later reading. A basket on the floor reveals a far greater subscription list, however. I spotted a surprising variety of publications: British and American *Vogue, Time, Vanity Fair, Harpers & Queen, Tatler, The Economist, Newsweek, Women's Wear Daily* and *Architectural Digest*! I questioned whether she truly read them all. 'You would be surprised at how much time you have to read in a 30-day period', she said. 'In taxis, planes, during breaks in the day, while soaking in a bath, while waiting for someone or before falling asleep . . .' I believed her!

Besides reading, Elizabeth, an executive wife of a property developer, has also developed a daily system for debriefing. From the moment she rises, the radio is turned on. Whether she is having breakfast, doing floor exercises, getting showered and dressed, news of the day is all around to be seen and heard. She tells the story of a house guest who wasn't such a news junkie. The serene, polite, accommodating and genteel friend stormed into the kitchen one afternoon with her hands gripping the sides of her head while shouting out, 'How many times can you listen to the same damn stories?' Elizabeth is so accustomed to having news as background noise that she has grown immune to repetition. She often chooses to be doing several things at once. So she relies a great deal on media reports for current information. Of course, her busy schedule does not afford her the luxury of lounging around awaiting a favourite programme. Hence, she has made certain that each of her household staff can operate the VCR and diligently reviews television schedules for new programmes and documentaries of interest. At other times, she will have programmes audiotaped as well, for accessible listening in the car or on her Walkman while exercising the dog.

Jane, the wife of a stockbroker, learned of the news subscription service her husband's company had through their Quotron computer system. By punching in any subject-matter or name of a company, the latest news will appear on the screen just as on the wire services. By the push of another button, a print-out of the story follows. Each morning Jane made a point of talking with her husband's secretary, who would scan the data bank for what she thought would be of interest or need to the wife. Each week, Jane treated her to a special lunch at a favourite restaurant as a 'thank you' and to be further informed on office activities. So she, too, has found an efficient and effective way of gathering intelligence.

Another wife of a public relations executive has also turned to her husband's office general staff for assistance. Trade publications, newsletters and cuttings make their way to the executive secretary daily. She receives a debriefing phone call from the secretary at the end of the day while her husband is on his way home. But what is different about Frances is that she actually got involved in her husband's accounts – unofficially, of course. Frances has become the back-up slogan master of the firm's specific accounts. She made a conscious effort to challenge or outdo advertising slogans or jingles. It reached a point where her husband and his top executives would do a mock presentation in front of her before presenting the material to the official client. Frances has made herself indispensable to her husband's business.

Mary, meanwhile, has pursued her own career whilst being a 'corporate' wife to her husband, who runs a large chain of newsagents. Even though she is very much involved in running a small fashion house, she nevertheless works hard at being the perfect hostess. She maintains that it is essential for her to be well informed about current events and usually ensures that she listens to the breakfast television for news whilst she is getting ready for the day. If she is not entertaining in the evening, she will also listen again to the news programmes. 'This is more important than ever if John wants to entertain people from overseas,' she says. 'Just recently, we had people here from Japan to dinner and it helped me enormously knowing something about their culture.' Days previously she had topped up her knowledge by visiting the Japanese Embassy and had spent an afternoon reading up on their way of life, their traditions and their attitudes. 'I discovered that in so many ways, they think differently from us,' she explained. 'So to learn about their culture helped me to talk with them and understand them.'

Shirley is the twenty-six year-old wife of an oil company executive. She explained that without her daily reading of the national newspapers, she could not cope with the huge amount of entertaining she has to do. She quite openly admits to being a company wife, but says she enjoys it. 'As long as I've done my background homework and genned up on national and international current affairs, I can look forward to seeing and looking after my guests,' she says. Shirley considers that being the wife of a high powered man is a *job*, plain and simple. It is one which has to be done well and, as with all jobs, has to be worked at. She and her husband entertain clients in their magnificent Somerset country house almost every weekend during the autumn and winter months. 'I am used to passing strange people on the stairs,' she says. Unlike many other wives, she gave up a promising career in marketing when she married. Her knowledge of this subject, however, plus the information she gains from the media, enables her to feel confident most of the time and she says she enjoys the challenge of constantly meeting new people.

5

How to communicate effectively

'Speech is power,' Emerson said. 'Speech is to persuade, to convert, to compel.' Yet too many of us pay little attention to this very important issue. Your attitude, your actions, your expression and your overall presence reveal as much about you as the words you speak. When speaking to others, your goal is to emanate confidence. Your ultimate purpose becomes to state your point effectively so as to elicit the response you want. Lewis Carroll wrote in *Alice in Wonderland* that 'One of the hardest things in the world' is to convey meaning accurately from one mind to another. So when Alice said, 'Really, now you ask me, I don't think. . . .', the Mad Hatter responded appropriately, 'Then you shouldn't talk'.

A large number of companies spend fortunes in developing better communications systems. But until someone introduces the mechanical being that is able to think precisely, speak authoritatively, produce reports and memos that win friends and influence people, it rests upon you to do these tasks skilfully and graciously. When you think about it, communication is useless or even harmful unless what you say or write is properly interpreted. Although a company can spend a sizeable sum on modernising old equipment with technological/electronic/computerised systems, often little is invested in the individuals who are affected by it. So it remains important to remember that when it comes to your attitude, speech, conduct and appearance, the rules are clearly defined by etiquette's time-honoured standards and formalities. Hence you should not be faced with drastic communication barriers if you rely on the Queen's English, either spoken or written. Trends in jargon and idiom shift as often as fashions in clothes. The spoken or written word can last forever.

The words you speak as an executive or political wife are generally expected to be of a persuasive nature. No business-social function is for entertainment purposes only. It is always a public relations function designed to promote better relations, hopefully resulting in feelings of goodwill towards the executive and his company, and also in increased business. Thomas Mann, the great German novelist, has said that 'Speech is civilisation,' by which he apparently concluded that conversation is the only civilised and effective way to produce desired results.

The value of persuasiveness is not limited to high-risk, crucially important situations. You do not go through a single day without a real need for the ability to speak persuasively. Favours are to be gained, mistakes are to be forgiven, assistance is to be obtained, opinions are to be changed – thus the need for persuasive speech goes on and on. You cannot escape the necessity of persuasiveness, and those who do pay an on-going price. Just how valuable to you is the skill of persuasive speech? People are rarely free from desires, needs and opinions which clash either with objective reality or with the desires, needs and opinions of others.

It can be said that the continuing demand for persuasive skills is demonstrated most clearly by politicians. They have to develop the most penetrating skills in order to persuade the country to adopt their policies, which they also have to become used to being fervently questioned by fellow politicians and the media, as well as by the general public. In what some would call very adverse conditions, they are mercilessly questioned and that is when their persuasive abilities must be seen to be paramount. Politicians often have to persuade the general public that in order to make the country better, we have sometimes to endure hardship. This could not be more true than at the present time, when Britain has had to put up with very high interest rates in order to bring down inflation. Many companies have gone bankrupt because of this and unemployment ensues.

I was privileged to be involved in a political issue concerning the people of Hong Kong. Hong Kong is a British Crown Colony at present but this will cease in 1997, when mainland China will take over. Although it is established that all people living in Hong Kong are British, Parliament stipulated that it would be impossible to allow all the residents to come and live in Britain if they so desired. At the time, it became a very real issue and an organisation was formed in Hong Kong called the 'Hong Kong People' who were intend on persuading the British public to reverse their Parliament's decision.

We set up a campaign which was dedicated to achieving this. We interviewed many of the residents of Hong Kong and established how this state of affairs would affect them and their families, how the ordinary man in the street would react to being taken over by the mainland Chinese and what it would mean to him. These case histories were then brought to the attention of the media in the form of articles and many of them were printed by the national press. We then in turn interviewed the British people to ascertain their reactions to these human stories and likewise involved the national press to assist. The campaign was further strengthened by members of the opposition parties who had regular debates in Parliament on this matter. We brought in top level executives from Hong Kong, who had meetings with Mrs Thatcher and people of influence within the British business fraternity. Gradually, our persuasion campaign began to succeed, resulting in the Government agreeing to ensure that up to fifty thousand people resident within Hong Kong could come to Britain to live, if necessary. This is not a total success, as we would wish all residents to be able to have the choice, but by putting forward the views of the general public both in Hong Kong and in this country we were able to persuade Parliament to have a change of heart.

Regardless of the advantages or disadvantages you may possess due to your husband's position, you are entitled to the satisfaction of contributing to his success. This satisfaction is not too much to expect. Most of us have a bit of an uphill climb in mastering persuasive skills, but you can certainly work at gaining them.

The experts like to refer to 'psychological illiteracy' when it comes to fundamental aspects of human relationships. Our persuasive ineptitude is frequently startling. For example, a corporate wife may say, 'The reason I could not accompany Jack to the dinner was because I have friends from out of town to entertain'. Does she expect special consideration for an absence that she declares outright was caused by her giving precedence to another obligation? In a persuasive conversation, I find that people will often say, 'Do you know what I mean?' or 'Can you understand what I'm getting at?' This certainly questions the intelligence of your listener, doesn't it? It practically forces him or her to oppose you on the statement or issue you are making. It's simply a natural reaction in order to maintain self-respect.

Persuasive skills are very often more demonstrated by women than by men. I think most women are more sensitive to the needs of others and they can thus use diplomacy in dealing with those needs in order to achieve their own ambitions and those of their husbands. I have long since advocated that a businesswoman can open more doors just because she is a woman. Once her persuasive skills are used to influence a mere male that her company is better than her competitor's, he really doesn't stand a chance – such are her talents that the man in question will not only give in but will think it is his idea anyway!

Anabelle typified this reasoning, although when I first met her she was a young mother of two very small sons. She had given up her career as a creative artist in order to be at home with her two children. Her husband ran an advertising agency and at the time of our meeting, she was very distressed because she did not see much of her husband, she felt trapped at home and she was worried about her marriage. She and her husband seemed to be drifting apart. What made matters worse was the fact that her husband did not want her to work. He told her many times during their marriage that he and he alone would be the breadwinner and he did not want his children to grow up without their mother being always at home. No matter what Anabelle did, she could not convince him that she was desperately unhappy and now that the children were starting school, she felt she was becoming a cabbage because she had no interests.

When someone is as low as this, it is difficult to suggest that she try to find other interests to occupy herself during the day, such as sport, gardening or even improving her creative talents with art lessons at a part-time school. Anabelle was a bright, vivacious girl, but it was evident that she was becoming very introverted and had began that painful cycle of not going out and cancelling any future opportunities to do so. Gradually, she did not bother to put on her make-up each day, nor bother with her hair or her appearance generally. I am sure we have all known someone like this. Unfortunately, it is becoming a very well-known situation and statistics show that it happens to women far more than with men, often leading to bad drinking habits in order to blot out their unhappiness.

What Anabelle wanted more than anything else in the world was to work, but she did not want to upset her husband. She had tried many times in the past to persuade him that she should work in order to make her feel whole again. She had always been active in her world and had been employed as a creative artist by several advertising agencies as a freelance, prior to meeting her husband in one of these agencies and subsequently marrying him. When first married, she enjoyed being at home in her new house and choosing the colours and furniture to make it their own special home. Soon came her babies and life was very busy. Many of us wives will understand this situation all too well: it is only when the children grow up and go to school that suddenly life becomes very lonely.

Anabelle was still only twenty-five when we talked this through. I suggested she talked over the situation with her husband once again, but instead of becoming angry with him, she should try to persuade him to change his mind. She could ask him if he liked seeing her in this bleak situation. Would he not like the same lively girl he married back again? This would happen if only he would 'allow' her to take a part-time job so that she could still be there when the children returned from school. Her husband remained adamant that he would not consider any such compromise. He was very ambitious and, as a corporate wife, she was expected always to be able to entertain at the drop of a hat and to attend any company functions. She also used this as part of her persuasive argument that surely he could see she would be able to operate much better at these events if she had something more positive to say. He still said a definite no! No wife of his would go out to work. She came to us to have confidence lessons, and goodness knows she needed them. Her husband's attitude made what confidence she had slowly ebb away. At the same time, I introduced her to a friend of mine who ran a tennis club and she began to take up tennis enthusi-astically.

After about nine months or so, Anabelle came back to see us. This time she explained her husband was in financial difficulty with his business. During the boom years of his industry he had naturally thought that his company was indispensable to his existing clients and had extended his offices and staff accord-ingly. Unfortunately, advertising is one of the first things com-panies cut back on when they are in difficulties. This had happened to Anabelle's husband and he realised too late that he could not recover his losses. He sacked most of his staff and had to sell some of the office space in order to make ends meet.

He himself was despondent, but the good news was that he began to talk things over with his wife. Gradually, Anabelle began to learn more about his business and about his clients. She persuaded him to let her become involved with all his clients in the way we have already described that a good corporate wife should. By getting to know them and their families and through entertaining, she was able to assist her husband to create and maintain good business relationships. When a husband and wife work together in this way, it is truly a powerful force! It could be said that when there is a crisis, it is easier to persuade and such was the case with Anabelle.

During a company reception which she had helped to arrange, she was introduced to a man and wife who were a medical team. They later explained to her that they were very excited about their new product. It was a method of relieving pre-menstrual tension (PMT) in women and was taken not in tablet form, but in an oral spray. When taken it relieved tension and period pains almost immediately, and also built up a resistance to cope with them in the future months. How best should they promote this?

Anabelle was beside herself with excitement. She knew exactly what to do to promote this breakthrough, but would her husband let her? One of the basic principles to persuade anyone to your way of thinking is to obtain all the facts. With this in mind, Anabelle obtained everything she needed to know about this amazing product. She also worked on creating an effective corporate image, a logo, etc., suitable to the product, together with budget predictions and a business plan. Finally, everything was ready but would her husband let her operate the account and in her own way? She had to persuade him. This was her chance of a lifetime. We discussed together how best to approach him.

First she would identify with him, his needs and requirements. These must surely be that he would wish for more clients, more business. By ascertaining these, she could then persuade him to let her put her ideas into practice. Surely, he had nothing to lose and everything to gain? If the idea did not work out successfully, only a few people would be aware of this, but if they did prove successful, it would bring in more revenue. Armed with these persuasive tactics, together with all her other business material, she went home to 'pick the right moment' with her husband.

Her jubilation was there for all to see when she came to see us a week or so later. Her husband had reluctantly agreed and she was now busy preparing her campaign. She was a changed woman. By identifying her husband's needs first, she was easily able to persuade him rather than by arguing with him that by letting her obtain this contract, his own business would benefit accordingly. The campaign was successful and so began a husband-and-wife business partnership which has become a major influence in the advertising world today. Anabelle is now managing director of the company, with her husband as chairman. She has become a powerful businesswoman and her creative skills have been brought to the fore by creating many imaginative campaigns for her clients.

When we are surrounded by examples of persuasion like those I have mentioned, what is therefore important is greater understanding of human motives and an increased awareness of persuasive techniques. When we talk about persuasive conversation, it is not something strange to you, like learning to speak Russian or mastering micro-economics. You use persuasion every day of your life. But, more importantly, you have been subject to a steady diet of persuasive influences. Fortunately, no man, woman or child can ever be totally persuasive. That would be a power too far-reaching for anyone to be entrusted with. However, you certainly can expect to increase enormously your personal persuasive powers.

Most people agree that persuasion is any form of discourse

that influences thought, feelings or action. In a sense, most conversation can be considered persuasive because all speech can be classified as influential when you come down to it. Simply greeting someone with 'Good evening', or 'I am delighted to meet you', may at times be influential. Often a smile can be interpreted as persuasion, or indeed, your general manner towards people. How you greet people can be very persuasive. If someone is coming to your home and you greet them with a warm smile and open arms, you immediately have your guests eating from your hands, so to speak. By your very actions, you have persuaded them to think that they are the *only* people you wanted to see at that precise moment. You have made them feel at ease, comfortable and welcome. The fact that you are tired because the kids kept you awake all night or you are wondering if the beef for dinner is going to be too dry, has not affected your impact. Yes, it is all an act – theatre, if you like, but if this is what is required to make the difference between failure and success, it is well worth the effort. The added bonus is that you become extremely popular. People like and respect you. You become known for being the perfect hostess and the wonderful wife of your husband – a wife whom everyone wants to meet and to talk with.

One of my friends, Pam, has developed this to a fine art. Married to the chairman of a major accountancy company, she epitomises everything that is required to persuade anyone to do almost anything she wants them to do and feel very happy doing it. Her secret persuasion technique is to make everyone feel they are very special to her. We all want to be loved, to be made to feel special, and we warm to anyone who makes us feel so. Pam will always remember birthdays and remember to send flowers when she knows you are involved in a special event, such as a new birth. Friends, colleagues and her husband's clients all have the same treatment from her. Her husband now realises that her 'talent' for making each person feel good can help him win clients. Although, of course, he is very able at his profession, it has already been noted that his clients very often are 'persuaded' by her in this subtle way to join him rather than his competitors.

The main reason that I want to distinguish *persuasion* from other forms of speech is because of the conscious purpose of your remarks. At absolutely any company function you attend, whether a day at Ascot with a multitude of people, or dinner with your husband and a client, you are there for a specific purpose. Even in the most informal circumstances, you must never forget what is your primary relationship to the people present. Often I have heard executives say that they closely examine the behaviour of peers or subordinates after a long day, a tiring trip or while on a holiday, for that is when their true character prevails. Anyone can master a performance for so many controlled hours a day, but watch a person under stress and strain and his true colours emerge soon enough. Therefore, in most things you say, you will be making a calculated effort to change the perception or orientation of your guest or host. Your purpose in conversing will be to render your listener different, in belief, in attitude, in feeling, in action. It may be as minor as requesting a lunch date or suggesting a new Thai restaurant, or as major as landing that crucial account.

All corporate wives should endeavour to become expert persuaders! They can accomplish so much by using these techniques to assist their husbands to acquire new clients. A wife who knows how to capitalise on this ability can also establish the knowledge which is required in order to maintain or improve a business relationship with his colleagues or existing clients. Let me explain . . . Take, for example, the company wife I know whose husband was very anxious to draw a particular person into his business, possibly as a partner. The husband had 'headhunted' this man whom he thought would be ideal for heading a new computer division of the company and, at the time, felt that no other person would do. He had duly 'courted' him for many months, offering what appeared to be an excellent salary and good working conditions as well as the use of a good relocation service. All these efforts, however, proved unsuccessful.

Sarah had listened for many hours to her husband and to his absolute conviction that to acquire this man would improve his business two-fold. After thinking out her techniques, she suggested to him that he invite the man and his wife to dinner at home. At the same time, she requested her husband not to talk too much about work and his business; this occasion would simply be seen as a social occasion to get to know one another.

The evening duly came and all went well. Sarah quickly established that the man and his wife were very happy in the home they had created over the years, which was many miles away from her husband's business. She also learned that they had two boys, aged ten and eleven. With this in mind, Sarah began telling them of her delight that her son, who was twelve, had started school within the area and that it was recognised as one of the best schools in the country. Their success rate for examination passes was well known. She went on to talk of their ambitions for their son and, as she did so, she could see how eager the wife had become. She began asking Sarah questions about the school and about the teachers. Once the evening was over and they had said goodnight to their guests, Sarah turned to her husband and said: 'It's in the bag!' Sure enough, approximately one week later, the wife asked Sarah if she could arrange a time for her to see the school. As a result they moved to the area and to the husband's company very shortly. By using her persuasive skills, Sarah was able to ascertain the couple's needs and desires for their sons which led to the man's decision to become eventually a partner in the company.

As I have stated, persuasion is that form of conversation which attempts to influence someone else. But it has been my experience that many women who are not experienced in this sometimes confuse persuasion with argument. It certainly is a related, but much more restricted, form of speech. The main difference between persuasion and argument is one of *method*. Both are trying to gain influence: using persuasion which Aristotle described as 'all available means' to get the message across, as opposed to argument, 'reasoned discourse', which uses facts and logic to influence your listener in any and every way possible. Basically, argument appeals to your thinking abilities, whereas persuasion focuses on facts, logic, emotions and rationalisation. Another important distinction is that argument usually starts with a specific and clear statement of what you want to accomplish. But persuasion typically attempts to lead the reaction of your listener in a desirable direction before you reveal your specific goal. Argument has also too often been known to become 'heated'. Persuasion, on the other hand, is usually non-controversial. Effective persuasive conversationalists use their appeals as baits and lures to gain the upper hand.

A client of mine spoke of his wife as being argumentative – meaning she was combative whenever she spoke. But he referred to himself as persuasive – meaning that it is difficult to find any reason for wanting to disagree with him! If argument is in any way like war, persuasion is more like commerce – where both buyer and seller have something to gain.

I observed an ideal example of this some years ago. My client, as chairman of a manufacturing company, was in negotiation with the Nigerian government over a very large contract. The initial talks had gone well and his team had made many presentations. The time had now come to sign the final contract. It became known that the Prime Minister and his government officials were to spend some days in Geneva and the Nigerian Minister of State suggested that if my chairman would like to see them, the following weekend would be an ideal opportunity to discuss further details. My client asked me to arrange this and as the Minister had made known that he would like to get out of Geneva for the weekend, I searched for the right venue. I felt it had to be reasonably quiet so that talks could take place easily and throughout the whole of the weekend's activities, rather than constantly sitting in a room. Also, the Nigerian Ministers had indicated that they wanted to get away from the sophistication of the Swiss hotels.

Eventually, I found what I considered to be a perfect spot. It was in the little village of Talloires set deep in the mountains and near Lake Annecy. The hotel had been a monastery, built in 1764. The wonderful oak beams and superb oak staircases added grace to the equally beautiful rooms. The beauty was further enhanced by the superb wine cellar and food. It had been awarded five Michelin stars, which meant that the experts agreed this was certainly a place to visit. I spoke to my client and explained that the hotel was simple but charming and the quality of food and wine second to none. He agreed we would spend the weekend there with our guests, but that I should book one entire floor for the Prime Minister alone.

As the Nigerian guests arrived, I was relieved to see that they were as excited about it as I had been. Everything appeared well until I took the Prime Minister to his floor. He gazed first in amazement and then anger when he realised that he had the entire floor to himself. He turned to me and said 'I only wanted a bed, you know.' I felt very bad over his remarks, especially when I could see that his anger remained throughout the morning. The chairman told me that the morning meetings had gone very badly.

Next came lunch. We were all anxious that this at least could be successful, and indeed when the menus were brought to us, there in front of us was a magnificent selection of the most coveted dishes cooked splendidly, accompanied by magnificent wines. The chairman looked at the Minister and asked what he would like. 'I would like a toasted cheese sandwich!' he replied. Well, the faces of the chairman and his team were a sight to be seen. Here was the best the world could offer and all he wanted was a cheese sandwich! This incident led to a very strained luncheon and again the Prime Minister looked angry and did not take part in the table conversation.

Early that evening, before our guests came down to dinner, the chairman and I discussed the situation. Something was dangerously wrong. Was it the venue? Were the terms of negotiations not in order? Had he offended the Minister in any way through the terms of the contract? We just did not know the answer and the evening had to continue under this very big cloud. I was privileged to be seated next to the Prime Minister that evening at dinner and during conversation, I discovered he was a Cancerian. I too am Cancer born and we laughed about being two Cancerians together and compared notes on how we react to certain situations. I really do not know whether it was because we both were born under the same birth star or not, but we somehow felt we had empathy with one another and later that evening, we found ourselves chatting away about life in general.

When my client had retired to bed eventually I found the opportunity gently and, I must say, rather cautiously to ask the Minister about the hotel and his reaction to it. He told me quite precisely that in view of the accommodation he had been given, plus various other factors, he felt he had been patronised. Rather than being pleased with it, he was very angry and this in turn was affecting all business matters. He explained that he and his colleagues were from a poor country and one of the reasons they had asked to come away from Geneva was to enjoy a more relaxed and simple weekend. He had come from a very humble background and, rather than enjoying the magnificence of a whole floor to himself, he found it distasteful and would have preferred an ordinary 'simple' room such as his colleagues had. He had completely misread the situation and it made me realise all too well that it is often these apparently simple things which can affect business and indeed world affairs.

The following morning, I spoke to my client early before the others emerged. I explained to him about our conversation and said that the venue was right but the way we were using it was not. We could not now take the Minister from his suite and give him a more 'simple' room, but at least we could arrange other activities to make him feel better.

From that moment on, the whole weekend structure changed. I hired small boats for us to sail on the beautiful Lake Annecy. We had picnics by the water's edge. We dressed casually to do all this and gradually the mood of the weekend changed to enjoyment and, whilst business was constantly discussed, we all seemed to be in a pleasant mood, soaking up the magnificent scenery amid snow-capped mountains. I can only assume that the Minister's anger had subsided as he took an active part throughout the rest of the weekend. Because of his anger, however, the consequences of having a completely different and relaxed couple of days meant that we all enjoyed the time in Talloires so much more. By using these methods of persuasion, we were able to recapture the good business relationship which had previously existed between my client and the Nigerian government and which has continued.

Many years ago, I came across a book entitled, *The Human Use of Human Beings*. Needless to say, the title caught my attention. The author said that 'speech is a joint game between the talker and the listener against the forces of confusion'. The 'major opponent' of 'normal communicative discourse', he said, 'is the entropic tendency of nature itself'. Entropy, as Webster explains it, is 'a mathematical measure of unavailable energy'. So here we have it, a huge amount of natural energy that is plainly not available to us. The author continued: 'It is not the quantity of information that is sent that is important for action, but rather the quantity of information which can penetrate into a communication and storage apparatus sufficiently to serve as the trigger for action.'

In reality, it's all simple stuff and common sense. Persuasion simply becomes the method of speech that you decide to use in order to make your point clear and understood, while gaining empathy and support from those to whom you are speaking. It is a diplomatic way of winning them over. A colleague of mine in the public relations profession knew how to do just that by carefully focusing on what she refers to as 'selective attention'. The things we do, the way we live is determined by what we choose to notice. We see what we want to see and basically ignore everything else. So obviously, the contact we have with other people and events is determined by the decisions we make – through selective attention. After all, to be human is to be highly selective, to be oriented towards interests, particular people, chosen events.

So then, the main purpose for you, the persuasive conversationalist, is to focus on the selective attention of your listener. What interests them? How do you build on that in order to gain a favourable outcome for yourself? Your basic and vital approach is to gather the wandering thoughts of your listener and to get him to focus on the issue you have in mind. Your target should be left with the impression that it was all mostly his idea. You should leave with the promise that your mission is on the verge of being accomplished.

A client of mine put this into practice recently. As the wife of a politician, she had come to us because she needed her confidence boosted. After going through our confidence techniques, she then decided to lose some weight, and had a new hair style – a complete new image – and with her newly found confidence, she was enjoying the social side of being the wife of an eminent politician. However, her new image made her want her husband to consider a change too! She realised that they had both become overweight and as she had done something about herself, her husband's flab seemed all the more obvious. She also wanted to change his style of suits and to stop him from wearing very loud ties. He thought that if he wore bright coloured ties, for example, he was very much 'with it'. Instead, they had the reverse effect. He said he did not want to lose weight as he enjoyed his food too much. Unfortunately, politicians have to eat at odd hours and mostly late at night, which is totally the wrong time.

My client then began what can only be described as a very devious campaign. She knew that the more she asked him to change, the more determined he was not to do so. So she began by discussing her worry about his weight to a couple of medical friends and it was agreed that they would take every opportunity to tell him how dangerous it was to be overweight. This was to be carried out in a casual, almost off-hand manner, simply to alert him to the fact.

The House of Commons has a keep-fit club for the use of MPs day and night between sessions. She discovered a new club was soon to be replacing the old one, with more modern equipment, and she made sure that she and her husband had an invitation to attend the opening. When her husband finally agreed to attend, she also arranged for the organisers to demonstrate their new assessment equipment in front of the audience at the opening. This assessment told individuals what, if anything, was wrong and how to plan to put it right and eventually to become fit. As arranged, who should they pick on to demonstrate this . . .? Yes, you've guessed it! The poor man was told in no uncertain manner and in front of his fellow MPs that he should definitely lose weight. They would devise a programme for him to do so immediately. He really found he could not get out of this at all, as his colleagues constantly asked him during the following week how much weight he had lost. In front of them all, he had promised to do something about it, so he had to carry it out. On reflection, my client felt sorry for him, but knew this was the only way to make him aware of the fact that his overweight not only looked bad, but was not at all good for his general health. However, the desired action took place and she persuaded him through other people to lose that weight.

Gradually she gently persuaded (not nagged!) him to buy new, more stylish suits to fit his new, slim body. Whilst accompanying him when buying these, she would also request the outfitters to suggest a shirt and tie to go with the suit and insisted on buying these herself for him. So there was no getting away from it. She tells me she has now been able to throw out all the loud ties and although he still complains, he hasn't bought any others. Can you imagine both of them out walking with their new images after over forty years of marriage with the old? Persuasion can be fun, but sometimes costly too, as my client's husband discovered.

Remember that whatever captures one's interest will influence their behaviour. So when you are speaking to someone in a persuasive manner, you are influencing their actions towards your ideas and away from the alternatives. When you have someone's interest and attention you have their belief, their willingness to act, their acceptance of your point of view. Attention and interest are words that, although not synonymous, are constantly related. We always give our attention to things we find interesting. It's a natural reaction. Interest grows with familiarity, with knowledge, with prolonged attention to something or someone. Therefore, you capture someone's attention in a conversation by finding some common ground on which you can build your case. You arouse his interest by a means that is partly physical and part mental. Attention can become 'breathless' where the pulse rate increases, muscles sometimes stiffen and the endocrine glands work overtime as you observe your listener while talking to him. His consciousness is drawn, as if by supernatural power, towards the main points of your conversation. If, on the contrary, he is bored and appears not to be paying too much attention to you, his eyes will wander, he may listen to distracting sounds or someone else's conversation and his body may slouch or slump in his chair. His mind is elsewhere. If you do not know what state your guest is in, then you obviously need to sharpen up your observation skills as well.

Joanne had just such a problem when she came to see me. She was very unhappy, as she and her husband were going through a bad patch in their marriage. Joanne was rather different from many of the wives who attend our courses. She had four children, and when the youngest was about ten her husband's company went bankrupt. He took this very badly indeed and had a nervous breakdown. Joanne faced the fact that they would have virtually no money unless she, herself, went out to work. She found a job working in a television studio and started thoroughly to enjoy her work. She also changed from being a rather frumpy fair girl to a glamorous blonde.

After about a year, she became aware that a new position within the studio was to become vacant. In the past, she had been involved very much behind the scenes as a secretary. The new position was one in front of the cameras, detailing the weather. If she was accepted, she would appear on breakfast-time television giving the reports on the weather every half hour and would be quite high-profile. She was very excited about the prospect. However, when she approached her boss who was also in the position to offer her the new job, he was not convinced that she was able to do it. He simply would not listen long enough to allow her to justify why she thought she was suitable. Each time she spoke to him, he would start to do other things, he would not look at her and he would end the conversation abruptly. Worse, he began advertising for someone else to take the position.

Many would have given upon being faced with this situation but, unlike many of the wives who came to see us, she had confidence, and lots of it. She was determined to persuade her boss that she was the right one, after all, for the job. Could we help? My assistant who does the camera interviews at each course, came to the rescue. She and Joanne spent hours together in front of the television camera practising methods on how to react. They made up mock weather reports and set up a map, and each day Jo would go through her paces with the camera.

After a very short time, when every spare hour had been taken up with the exercises, Jo told us it would have to be now or never, as already two other people had been contacted and were due for interviews shortly.

Her boss was young, ambitious and very dynamic. One morning she knew he had to attend a management meeting which would take up most of the morning. When he returned, she had positioned her map on the wall in his office and was waiting for him with her 'pointer' at the ready. As soon as he reached the door, she started giving out a weather report just as she had rehearsed in our office. Her boss stopped short and stared at her. Suddenly, she said afterwards, 'I had all his attention'. He sat down in a chair opposite and really listened to what she was saying and how she was promoting herself. When she had finished, he came towards her and put his arm round her shoulders. 'That certainly deserves a try at the real thing,' he said and went on to arrange some 'takes' for approval.

I am pleased to say this does have a happy ending. Yes, Jo did get the job, but not for very long. She now hosts a small television afternoon programme, and had time out to have another baby. Her persuasion skills were perhaps a little over the top, but they worked for her and they can work for you.

6

How to get into, or on top of, conversation

You are seated at the table in your navy velvet designer gown. Next to you is a cigar-puffing, champagne-drinking giant of a man. He looks you over and as if to relieve you of utter boredom, pontificates on an issue of the day. You are certain that he is a used car salesman: an imposter hoping to avoid exposure. How did he get here? 'Dear,' he begins, 'city planning has gone out of the minds of men and onto the disks of computers . . .'

You instantly decide this one is not worth nurturing, and nip it in the bud. 'It's not so unusual, is it?', you reply. 'You do recall that Baron Haussmann had the help of the mathematician Jean Charles Alphand in planning Paris. In fact, the boulevards were deliberately made a certain width to prevent the building of revolutionary barricades.' No, of course, he does not remember! This is absolutely *all* you know about the subject matter, but, as expected, the man does not have follow-up questions.

As a woman, you find that you must be able to keep up with sophisticates, put down the phonies, converse with scholars and survive . . .! Now, you can't be expected to know all the ins and outs of successful conversation the whole time, but you can learn enough to get through when necessary. Initially, you may not feel too comfortable about this practice, but familiarity will lessen your fears. There are rules and codes in the art of conversation as in all other things. Both content and delivery need to be focused on for desirable results. Combined with your personal style, you are practically guaranteed success.

We speak about confidence at many different levels and this is also crucial when it comes to speech in particular. If you don't come across as sounding sure of yourself, your credibility may be doubted. It isn't important whether or not you *are* an authority on the subject matter, but whether or not you *sound* as if you know what you are talking about is. For instance, if you mispronounce a certain word or phrase, you have the ability to make your listener think it is *he* who has got it wrong all along!

Most successful conversation is best conducted with short, decorative sentences. Don't say 'If the weather holds out, my mother will come and stay with the children so that Edward and I will be able to take a little holiday'. Instead, you say, 'Edward and I will be in St Tropez next week.' Your listener will not remember your mother, the kids, the little holiday. He will recall your enthusiastic statement about a week in St Tropez! He will not remember you as an indecisive, unsure and unconfident woman, but as a dogmatic, assertive one.

When I was a junior manager at an hotel in Bristol, I was delighted when, after a couple of months of lugging bottles of wine to the various bars when they ran out of stock, or helping to make beds when the hotel was short of staff, I was suddenly promoted to assist the banqueting manager. I enjoyed this job very much as I had to meet the people who came to the hotel wanting a function arranged, such as a dinner or wedding. Then, I would carry this through by assisting the banqueting manager in arranging all the details to make it a successful event. The flowers, the menus, the food, the wedding cake, place names, gifts for the ladies and so on . . . I remember many happy moments during these days especially when, on the day of the function, I could see all the details coming together and shared in the people's enjoyment of their own particular event.

However, I remember equally vividly one of my first days at this job when I met a guest at the hotel who wanted to have his annual dinner arranged there. On this occasion the banqueting manager accompanied me as I spoke to the man about his requirements. Obviously, I was a bit nervous, especially as he was rather an abrupt, almost rude man. The dinner was for a group of businessmen who were members of a social club called The Elephant Club. This particular year was the tenth anniversary and the guest asked me if we could arrange for an elephant to appear during the evening. I said that I did not know if we could do this and looked rather helplessly at the banqueting manager for help. He immediately intervened and said that of course he could get an elephant for this special occasion. After the man had gone, I couldn't wait to ask him where on earth was he to get an elephant! He told me that he had no idea where to get one. When I reminded him that he had told the guest he could get the animal, he replied 'Of course I did. You always tell the guest what he wants to hear. Never say you don't know.'

Later, I began to understand his psychology. People will accept most things if you tell them in an authoritative and forthright manner. If, for example, he could not get an elephant, he would tell the client that an elephant would make a mess at the dinner, or that it might trample the guests, or that an elephant was very expensive to hire. So the client would then appear to make the decision not to have the non-existent elephant and change to something else, happy in the knowledge that the banqueting manager was true to his word. People like authority and respect it. They build confidence from it. Some would say this example is downright dishonest but by going along with the banqueting manager's idea initially he, the guest, was confident that everything else would be handled in a professional manner. Saying that I did not know would undermine that confidence and make the guest slightly unsure of all the other details being dealt with in order to make his dinner a success. The cardinal sin is not to lie, but to say you don't know! Incidentally, we *did* get an elephant from the local zoo. The magnificent animal was gently led into the banqueting hall and up to the top table to the guest who had requested an elephant, whereupon he suddenly put out his trunk and ate the guest's entire dinner in one easy movement!

As you move around the social circuit, you find that people repeat what everyone else already knows. Don't get caught up in it yourself and become a bore. Be different. Become a master of the obscure and you won't have to be an authority on every issue. Did you ever hear anyone who did not have an opinion on Andrew Lloyd Webber's latest play or personal adventure? Mention that it certainly was no whim of fate that he married Sarah Brightman on the day of the Royal Gala opening of *Starlight Express* in London, so that he could present her to the Queen that night, guaranteeing extra coverage and impact for the show in the media. Isn't Donald Trump's ego always a topic whenever his name is brought up? Tell the story of Donald as a little boy from Queens – a poorer part of New York. His father was a low-income housing developer, but made a notable contribution to the building of the town's important bridge. During the ribbon-cutting ceremony the Mayor stood at a podium and publicly thanked everyone who was involved with the project. However, he forgot the name of one person – Fred Trump. That day young Donald swore that no one would ever forget the Trump name again!

Sometimes, an uncomfortable social situation will require that you make an especially short and concise statement so as not to prolong the agony. A young attractive former client of mine recalls the time when she was taken by her fiancé, a prominent doctor, to Geneva to meet the chief of staff of a famous research facility of which he hoped to become a member in the near future. You can imagine the anguish and turmoil she experienced during that ride from the airport to the hotel suite. But she decided to put a bold and brave front on it and charm the gentleman completely, providing she could prevent her teeth and knees from rattling too loudly, of course. Sometimes she lived by the words her friends bestowed upon her: 'Amanda, you are more brave than smart!', they would claim.

She rifled through jam-packed suitcases of clothes that evening and decided on a cranberry red double-breasted jacket and slim skirt by Ungaro. She wore sheer black stockings and snakeskin high-heeled shoes. An hour later Amanda was escorted to the residence of The Boss . . . and the entire party ascended to a smart Italian restaurant. Dr Kelton obviously admired the young woman and had difficulty diverting his attention away from her. At first Amanda was flattered, then embarrassed. She couldn't get through her dinner. Dr Kelton had fixed a frozen stare upon her across the table and, whether unconsciously or not, would not look away.

Amanda caught his eye and smiled briefly. She looked away to the side. He followed to see what she was looking at – his wife eating diligently. She turned back. He stared again. Well, Amanda thought to herself, if this is a showdown, then I'm going to give him a run for his money! With a fork stiffly positioned in her hand over the poached salmon, she stared back. No blinking. What appeared to be an eternity came to pass.

'Dr. Kelton,' Amanda finally broke the silence, but still without batting an eyelash or moving a muscle.

'Yes,' he replied.

'You know what Freud said about people who stared at each other for sixty seconds or more?'

'What?' he asked.

'They will go to war' (or make love, but she left that part out hoping he knew) 'and since you are much too kind a man to suffer defeat, we'd better not.'

He burst into laughter, relaxed enormously and has held Amanda in high esteem ever since.

Calling upon the past has many wonderful uses. Dr Kelton can check upon Freud, but chances are that he won't! Most people are aware of what is happening around us in the world today. They probably watch the same programmes or read the same items in the press. It's all crucial to know, but wouldn't you also like to turn to history for spicing up conversation? Sometimes, looking to the past where all is cobwebbed can be more effectively intimidating. History is murky. That's why we like it.

Another angle to consider in conversation is to focus on an issue or subject that you know enough about to be considered almost an expert. Of course, you are an expert on something obscure or out of the ordinary!

I know an executive wife who lives near a magnificent golf course. Her husband and his friends and colleagues make frequent use of it, but she has never swung a club herself although always accompanies them. Barbara has a variety of interests and this makes her well informed. She's one of those naturally curious people. She is simply horrified at the thought of participating in what appears to her a dull and unimaginative sport, but she nevertheless was intrigued by its history and the great tales that were told. So Barbara found her niche! She couldn't entertain her husband's guests on the golf course, but she certainly had them all spell-bound with historical anecdotes about the sport. They thought she only bluffed her lack of interest in golf because she told her tales with great zest and enthusiasm. She had become a true performer.

So with great drama and flair, Barabara would begin one of her amusing stories: On 6th March 1457, an Act of Parliament of King James II sternly warned Scotsmen 'That fut ball and golfe must be utterly cryit dune'. As far as we know, this is the first official mention of the game. It showed that the sport had a solid foothold in Scotland and was most likely played for more than a century without arousing official notice. Bureaucracy! The authorities had become alarmed over the strange fad that threatened to take the people's interest away from archery. Golf, therefore, found its way onto the dreaded prohibited list!

The king meant business, she would continue. There were laws against playing on the Sabbath. Then these laws were amended to forbid golf on Sundays. Tariffs were imposed on golf balls imported from Holland. But need we say that the Scots were stubborn? They proceeded to hack away over the heather and dunes with their knobbly sticks and feather-stuffed balls. Such a flagrant defiance of authority resulted in stiffer action by Parliament in 1491. The new law declared that not only would a fine and imprisonment be imposed on the avid golfer, but also a fine and jail sentence were to be inflicted upon those on whose property the renegades were found. Well! Opposition to this was taken up with King James IV immediately, not only by commoners, but also by nobility. Barbara then claims that she agrees with the king who has said that golf was a ridiculous sport, requiring neither strength nor skill and should properly be abandoned.

Barbara could entertain with stories from Jack Nicklaus all the way back to Adam. Yes, she is convinced that Adam too played golf in the Garden of Eden. He most likely fashioned a club from a surplus rib and entertained himself by swinging at apples from one tree to another. Eve, the first golf widow, out of despair and loneliness, resorted to the forbidden fruit . . . !

Barbara knows the importance of relying on 'authorities'. The use of authorities is an important aspect of conversation. It lends support to what you are saying. It offers evidence and suggests that those greater than the ones present agree with what you are saying. A famous name, a prestigious publication or organisation should always be within your mental grasp whenever the occasion calls for it. The greater the 'name', the greater the effect. This will take a little getting accustomed to but once you become familiar with the usage, the practice will become a reliable ally.

I have a wonderful friend who is extremely good at doing this. When she is telling you about a project or something she has done or a place she has visited, you can be sure she will always mention a Most Important Person. She is always involved in an endless round of charity meetings and committees and usually is asked to chair these, as she has a very forceful manner and can hold a committee together very well. These committees though, all seem to have one thing in common – the VIPs are always there as part of it. Somehow, somewhere there is always a Lord or Lady, or Viscount, Baronet or Knight. If they have not got a title then you can rest assured they will be president of an organisation or head of an authority. She is drawn to them like a moth to a flame. Consequently her conversation always sounds very authoritative and important, as her opinions are seemingly endorsed by the top people. They appear to give strength and credibility to her arguments and comments. She has developed this into a fine art and it is one which seems to work well.

Sometimes however, she really does go over the top! For example, she recently attended a dinner for one hundred and fifty guests where the prime minister, John Major, was the guest speaker. I overheard her saying to another friend 'I must dash. I'm having dinner tonight with John Major!' She *was* indeed having dinner with him, but she forgot to mention that so were a hundred and forty-nine other people!

When all else fails, a young writer friend of mine who finds that she is constantly dealing with considerably older and more worldly people, resorts to using words in unfamiliar contexts. She doesn't care about what it all means. The enigmatic angle of her statements separates her from the crowd. She comes across as an individual who is highly intuitive and perceptive. Who else would say, 'The play is a multi-disciplinary macrosystem *pour le sport* of verbal jousting'!

Similarly, the husband of a client of mine has developed the art of stopping people in their conversational tracks by saying something which is totally unexpected. With just one, finely-tuned remark, he will make everyone stop and look at him in amazement. But in some peculiar way, it also makes him appear very confident and forceful. It can also be used as an ideal

71

method of stopping boring people, as they do not usually like to be questioned in this way. For example, at a recent reception everyone was engaged in the usual 'small talk'. A VIP lady (probably on a committee with my friend!) was busily telling us how annoyed she was with 'today's young people'. The reception was a rather formal affair and one at which the Princess of Wales was the guest of honour. On such occasions, the men are usually requested to wear formal black tie and the women, long dresses and sometimes long gloves as well. A few of the younger people attending, however, were wearing slight variations of this. The men wore red or blue ties, for example, whilst the girls were in short cocktail dresses. The VIP lady was becoming very irate at what she described as 'the beginning of the end of another national tradition' and went on to say how difficult young people were. Suddenly my client's husband said sharply, 'Why?' The VIP stopped, stunned that her views were questioned in this manner, and there appeared to be a long awkward silence. Eventually, she gathered her thoughts together and tried to explain more fully the reasons behind her remarks. But the thread of thought had gone and the conversation moved on to other things.

I noticed that my client's husband was indeed a man of few words. He disliked small talk but he seemed to be very popular. He came across as very sincere, with a real sense of humour. I have met him on many occasions and because he uses this method of short, sharp words, people assume he is extremely confident. I know for a fact, however, that he is not nearly as confident as one imagines but has simply devised this approach and found it works. However, please beware if you decide to use the same method. It needs a lot of practice and the timing of your words must be absolutely right for it to be effective.

At other times, all one can do is make use of utter snobbery. How often has someone tried hard to impress by insisting that once he has experienced the best, everything else is just passing time or filling a void. I overheard a man who was a classic car enthusiast tell a lady that the only mode of transportation should be a Bristol Mark II, or else just opt for the horse and buggy. 'I don't agree,' she replied. 'I always preferred the convertible VW!' You win the upper hand by making your listener think that you are so knowledgeable and constantly exposed to 'the best' that you choose and prefer the simple and common!

An advertising friend is like this. When he was a high-flying executive on his way up to bigger things, he could not wait to buy the biggest house in the very best location just outside London. After a number of years and much hard work, he eventually achieved this by buying a beautiful manor house near Windsor. His was the place to go when he and his wife invited you to one of their lavish parties. Expense was not spared and they entertained very often. They would invite leaders of both the social and business worlds for weekend parties and one wondered how he had time to do any work at all with the number of parties he arranged. There were always people in his house. His wife was very tolerant and for many years worked alongside her husband to arrange the events and to entertain their guests. With two small children as well, she was obviously very busy most of the time. They seemed to be a good team together.

One weekend, however, she told her husband that she just had to get away for a few days in rural peace and tranquillity. He agreed to go with her and they simply jumped into the car and drove off, not knowing where they would spend the next few days. They thought that if they saw somewhere they liked, they would stop for the night. On the second day, whilst driving through country lanes, they came across a beautiful small house nestling in the trees, on a hillside offering magnificent views of the Cotswold hills. The house was derelict and had only one bedroom, no bathroom and a very small kitchen. My friend loved it immediately! He couldn't wait to talk to the people who owned it to see if they would sell. Of course, with his selling techniques, he had bought the house within a month and he and his wife moved in to make it a home.

All their friends said, perhaps rather patronisingly, that of course it would make a wonderful weekend retreat. Imagine their surprise when he said, 'We intend to live here permanently.' No one can understand his complete change of heart, but he and his family extended the house, but only slightly, so as to accommodate only them, and still maintain the house's beauty. And they *did* live there permanently!

After they had sold their Windsor manor house, there was no

room for any guests at their country cottage. Was this done on purpose, we all wondered? Was he now weary of people always wanting to call? Meanwhile, he commuted each day to the office in his blue Rolls-Royce and returned each evening to the peace of the countryside. He also became very much more relaxed. Recently he was having a conversation with some other business executives in my office. The others were saying how marvellous it was to live and work in London and they were slightly competing against one another as to the size of their houses. I was not too surprised to hear my friend say, 'I only have a very small cottage in the country.' Somehow, though, his relaxed confidence in stating this spoke volumes and left the others with the knowledge that, in some way, he had still outdone them!

On occasions, you may look up and discover that you have met your match. What's a girl to do? You're in a bind. There is no way out. The shark is swimming to the shore and he only sees . . . you! In this case, run for your life! Better flee than be discovered. Gently rub your throbbing temple and apologetically excuse yourself to see if the hostess can give you an aspirin. Discover the embarrassing ladder in your tights and dash to the ladies' room. Spot your long-lost Aunt Mildred across the room and simply tear yourself away to say hello. Anything you like, but just disappear!

This situation actually happened to me and it is a moment I will never forget! I had been asked by some friends to go to Antigua with them to look at the prospect of buying a small hotel there. We were going to spend some time exploring the hotels on offer and see to all the administration on site, but we were also looking forward to spending a few wonderful days enjoying this beautiful, unspoilt island. Patricia, my friend who had arranged the visit, knew many of the English people staying on the island as she had worked at the famous St James's Club in Antigua some years before.

One evening we were invited to a reception to be held at the St James's Club and my friend did not really want to go. Apparently, whilst she was an executive of the club, she had been treated rather badly by one of the male executives who had made her life hell and was the reason why she had left. He was organising this particular evening to encourage wealthy people to buy some of the beautiful villas with their own private beaches surrounding the club. The other friend who had come with us suggested that she or I should pretend to be someone who was *extremely* wealthy. After all, she said, no one knew us and we could have some fun with the man in question, thus giving some satisfaction to Patricia for the hard times she had put up with.

We were like three naughty schoolgirls as the other friend and I tossed a coin to see who should be the VIP. Well, of course, I lost so I had to be the one who would do it. We decided I should be known as Lady Diana de Courtney, who is well known for owning much property throughout the world and has many race-horses. We spent a great deal of time establishing what I should wear and decided on my plain black Yves Saint Laurent cocktail dress. With my tan, it looked simple but good and fitted the image we wished to portray. When we arrived at the club, I felt slightly nervous, but tried to look rich and arrogant! There were many famous people there, especially from the world of show business – Dudley Moore, Lisa Minnelli, Michael Caine, and many more.

The man from the club eventually introduced himself to me and, sure enough, he certainly put on all the charm. Nothing was too much trouble especially if I would consider buying one of the villas! I found I was quite enjoying being seen as a *very wealthy person*. People seemed to react differently towards me. Great wealth it seems is respected by everyone. Meanwhile, I discovered my two friends were mingling with the other guests and telling them who I was or, to be precise, who I was pretending to be! They had really entered into the game in a big way.

It was one of these people to whom they had been speaking, who suddenly appeared in front of me and introduced herself as 'Pamela'. She said she did not quite catch my name? 'Diana,' I replied. 'Is that Lady Diana de Courtney?' she questioned. 'Yes,' I said. She seemed to be amused and I became uneasy. Soon after, she drew me aside. 'You are Lady de Courtney from Oxford in England?' I nodded, knowing by now that something was wrong. 'That's funny,' she said. 'I'm her daughter, and you are certainly not my mother!'

Well, I could not speak! I was so embarrassed – what could I do? Where could I hide? Would she tell on me? I quickly grabbed my two friends together and gradually we explained what we were doing and why. Fortunately, she took it very well and laughed at our attempts to deceive everyone. I am pleased to say she helped us through the rest of the evening by telling everyone we were related, so our little ruse was not shown up for what it was. But it taught me a lesson – never to do this again. Although I have to say, I really did enjoy being a wealthy VIP for a few hours . . . !

All the activities shown in this chapter should be 'performed' with great ease, frankness of demeanour, a simple attitude. There is nothing deliberate or put-on about your delivery. Every remark you make – however calculated – comes through in a casual, unrehearsed way. Such remarks have stumbled into your brain effortlessly, the inevitable result of superior breeding and, of course, your superbly intuitive, perceptive and retentive mind!

7

How to know when actions speak louder than words

It was a glorious spring afternoon as a friend and I lunched together in a lovely outdoor setting. Susan is usually running at a hundred miles a minute on the inside, but she manages a cool and controlled exterior performance. We spent more than an hour enjoying our meal, the afternoon breeze and lively conversation. However, unbeknown to me, Susan had suffered from the stares of a gentleman seated several tables away. Since my back was turned to him, I missed the action, but others had certainly taken notice of the situation. The handsome stranger appeared perfectly content as he leaned into the chair with arms stretched out to the table, while nursing a cup of coffee and looking directly at Susan the entire time.

As we were getting ready to leave and walked towards the door, Susan stopped me and said, 'Excuse me for a minute.' Everyone watched as she walked over to the man's table, leaned over closely eyeball-to-eyeball and in a rather loud, affirmative voice asked, 'Are you going to miss me?' Expressions of shock, surprise and laughter filled the patio and I was of course, deeply puzzled by her course of action. Granted, Susan is a confident woman. But most people would respond to such a situation very differently, timidly perhaps, or even fearfully.

The direct, unwavering stare is interpreted as threatening by most people. Everybody at some time or another has experienced the uneasy sensation that they were being watched and closely observed by someone. Their intuition was always confirmed when turning round. The power of the disturbing stare has been noted all through history. Numerous cultures have told stories of the evil eye, the gaze that does harm to whomever it falls upon. A continuing belief claims that large staring eyes are definite magic. In the late 1940s ships that plied the Mediterranean still possessed a guarding eye on their prows. In the late 1950s, there was testimony before a United States Congressional Committee regarding an American businessman who hired a man to come in periodically and glare at his employees, an unspoken threat designed to keep them working diligently.

We have a built-in uneasiness when it comes to eye contact, because it increases intimacy, expresses and instantly elevates emotions and is a key element in sexual advancement. You can read the face of the man you encounter without meeting his eyes, but when your eyes meet not only do you know what he is feeling, but he knows that you know. Experience tells us that eye contact forces us to feel very exposed, raw and vulnerable.

I recall an occasion when I first started in business on my own. I had held quite a number of telephone conversations with a major industrial company which eventually led to an initial meeting with the marketing director. This was my first business meeting with my very own company and quite clearly I was nervous. I went through all the techniques of looking confident and tried on a number of outfits before I chose one which made me feel more so. I had previously studied body language too, in the hope that I would be able to learn how people reacted to me, how their actions would give me some clue as to what they felt about the service I was offering. Obviously, I also went through my presentation once again so that I was word-perfect – hopefully – and tried to convince myself that I knew my work well and that I would know the answers to any questions he was likely to ask. But the only thought which seemed to occupy my mind was that this man and his company *could* be my first customer!

I arrived on time for my appointment as I remember I had previously been told not to arrive too early, because this identifies immediately that you are too eager to please. The secretary duly ushered me into the manager's office and there I was, face to face with the man himself! I noticed he was younger than I had previously imagined, possibly in his early thirties. He shook hands with me and asked me to sit down in the chair he indicated. But I immediately noticed that he shifted his eyes away from mine when he spoke. He was courteous and politely led the conversation to the matter in hand. What had *I* to offer which was different from anyone else in the same business? I duly went through my presentation and he listened. I couldn't help noticing his body language, however. He always sat back into his chair, very casually, indicating that he was prepared to listen and with each arm resting on the arms of the chair, indicating that he was 'open' to any suggestion I might care to make. I also noticed that he would not look into my eyes. He would not look directly at me but his eyes mainly focused on the desk before him. I found this extremely difficult to cope with, as it gave me the impression that he was not interested in anything I had to say. Also, I found myself concentrating too much on making him look at me instead of on what I was saying.

My presentation was interspersed with questions from my listener and as it came to a close he began shifting himself in his chair. I waited for a response from him and suddenly he raised his head and looked me straight in the eyes. To my amazement I could see fear or nervousness in his gaze and felt that I must have misinterpreted this. Why should he be nervous? Surely, I had enough nerves for both of us! But the more he stared at me whilst discussing my work, the more certain I became that he was very nervous. I noticed that his body language had now changed. He began playing with his pen while he spoke. Later, when working for his company – yes, I did get the job – he and I became good friends. I discovered after some time that he had recently been promoted from a junior position within the company to that of marketing manager. I was one of the first consultants he employed for his company. Many years later, we laughed at the thought of how both of us were 'putting on an act' and trying to look and feel confident with one another. It was only when we had direct eye contact that we both knew how the other felt!

I focus on eye contact so strongly because, as you may already know, establishing eye contact or failing to establish it can change the whole meaning of an encounter. It is impossible not to make a powerful distinction between cutting a person off by pretending not to notice her, or cutting her off directly – seeing her, but refusing to take notice of her – which is a far more serious issue.

One of my clients had this happen to her, with disastrous results. As the wife of an executive in a team of financial analysts, her husband had just joined the company. After a number of months, he invited his wife, Anne, to meet the rest of his colleagues, including the company chairman. This did not unduly worry her as she was rather eager herself to get to know her husband's colleagues and to meet his boss. She had done her homework well on him and discovered that he was married with a young wife and two small children. He had started the company entirely on his own ten years ago and had built it up to become one of the most respected consultancies in the UK and the States. The reception was held in the company's main offices in Mayfair, in London's West End. Drinks and canapés were served and guests were invited to mix in order for staff and partners to become better acquainted. Anne seemed to fit in very well with the people she met from the company. Her husband's colleague were friendly towards her and she found she had a lot in common with several of the executives' wives as well as with some of his immediate working colleagues. As the evening wore on, she noticed that the chairman seemed to keep very much to himself. He appeared ill at ease. Eventually, she was aware that her husband was bringing him over to introduce him. She could not help noticing that he was a very large man – 6' 4" at least, and he towered above everyone else. As he was introduced, he briefly looked at Anne while shaking her hand.

Her husband began the conversation and led into the subject of children. He said that he and Anne had discovered that they and the chairman had children of the same age, and how difficult it was to cope with the very young. The huge man grunted some remarks in an uninterested manner and this was followed by silence! Trying to overcome the awkwardness of the situation, Anne spoke quickly to the chairman this time, complimenting him on his beautiful offices. As she did so, she was staggered to see that he simply spoke over her to another executive who had joined them, leaving Anne in mid-sentence! Completely ignoring her, he then introduced the newcomer to her husband and left. Anne's husband did his best to placate her by suggesting that perhaps his boss had not heard her in his attempt to bring one of his other employees to their gathering. Anne was not certain that this was the case, but was prepared to give him the benefit of the doubt.

A few months later, however, she attended another company event where the executives were entertaining clients at a golf tournament. She mixed with the guests in the marquee over-looking the eighteenth green on the course, and became involved in a conversation with another man who was a client of the company. She became engrossed in what he had to say and was suddenly aware of the chairman approaching them. Again, he more or less ignored Anne and, reaching for her companion's arm, began leading him away. The client was embarrassed at this and made some attempt to explain that he and Anne were in conversation. Not looking at Anne she heard him say to the client, 'She's only the wife of one of my executives. I want you to meet some more of my colleagues, all of whom are men!' The client stopped dead in his tracks. He looked at Anne, who by that time had her eyes filled with tears, and said to the chairman, 'If that is how you treat your employees' wives, then I am not impressed. Furthermore, because of your arrogance, I no longer want to do business with you!' For the very first time, the chairman looked at Anne straight in the face. The look, how-ever, showed extreme anger.

The client led Anne away, followed by her husband who by now knew something was wrong. Once the situation was explained to him, he also became very angry. The next day he handed in his notice. Meanwhile, his colleagues told him that the chairman did not like women. His wife rarely attended any corporate functions and he did not approve of women taking any part in business matters, and certainly did not like doing business with women executives. He was one of the few remaining men who still think the only place for a woman is in the home. By losing a good client, plus an excellent executive, he learnt to his cost that this no longer applies.

Eye behaviour is possibly the most subtle aspect of body language. Even in circumstances that provide only a fleeting eye contact, the sheer, cumulative amount of time someone spends looking at you implies specific things. The person you are talking to can in reality say a lot by the use of his eyes. If he glances away frequently while listening to you, he implies dissatisfaction with you. If he is looking away more than you feel is appropriate while he is talking, he then implies that he may be unsure about his statements or is altering them as he is going along. But if he is looking at you while listening, he is acknowledging agreement or offering his full attention. On the other hand, if he is looking at you while he is talking, he is showing his interest in how you react to what he is talking about.

I have a friend who does this constantly. He has the very disturbing habit of looking anywhere but at you when you are talking to him. He often looks for his cigarettes while you are talking. He also looks for his lighter, or he can't find any matches. If he is already smoking, he will shift constantly in his chair, look out of the window or fiddle with his notes. As I have known him for very many years, he often asks if he can have a cup of coffee right in the middle of our conversation and, of course, when it comes, he has to find a sweetener or he makes remarks to my secretary when she brings the coffee to him. He is infuriating!

Most people of course, consider him to be very rude, and they are right. But as I know him very well I have learned to understand that this constant movement and lack of attention is a form of his nervousness. Some would also say it is lack of concentration! However, this particular friend is equally infuriating when he is speaking to you. When he wants *your* attention, he demands instant attention by direct eye contact but is also extremely sensitive to your movements while he is talking.

For instance, my office overlooks a park. Situated in the heart of London, we are extremely lucky to have such a view. It is a wonderful sight to see the trees at any time of the year. In summer their superb foliage spreads so much that the trees seem to fight each other for space, and in the autumn the myriad colours are beautiful to behold. I have my desk near the window so that I can look at this beauty without moving from my chair. However, if I dare to look towards the park when my friend is talking, he will immediately refer to it and say I am not interested in what he has to say. Any other movement I may make, he interprets in the same way. He therefore demands that he has my complete attention at all times, otherwise he assumes I am not listening.

Another person I know of will not make any real preparations prior to a business meeting taking place. Most people usually prepare and rehearse what they have to say so that they feel confident enough to cope with any situation. He will not do this. He will be guided throughout by the movements, actions and eye contact of the person he is trying to impress. He explains that in this way, he is able to adapt what he has to say and the way he says it to fit in with the other person.

For example, let us assume that he has decided to be very aggressive and to present himself in a domineering way and with a loud, commanding voice. When he met the person whom he wished to impress and found that *he* was equally aggressive and loud, there would be an immediate conflict as each person tried to outdo the other. On the other hand, if he approached their meeting with an open mind, he could adapt his own attitude and manner to suit the other person's aggression and appear quiet but confident. Whatever manner he adopted would be determined by immediate eye contact with the other person. He would know exactly how to proceed once he had looked into their eyes and taken note of how they responded.

An individual's eye behaviour is often influenced by his personality, his life circumstances, his feelings and motives regarding those he is with and the business/social strata of those present. The man in charge of the conversation can in reality even control the actions of his listeners with the way he uses his eyes. This is demonstrated by politicians. When they want to make valid points on policy issues or their views on current affairs, they seek every opportunity to look squarely at their opponents and make direct eye contact with them. Mrs Thatcher became well known for doing this. On television many of her interviewers were completely overcome when she disapproved of some of their questions. She would lift her shoulders and look straight into the eyes of the interviewer and make her point whilst daring him to interrupt her! Similarly, when visiting other countries, many heads of state learned to avoid 'the look' during heated debates. Such was her strength that they realised she used her eyes to gain control.

John Major, as Britain's new prime minister, recently made a huge impact on the British public. He had been in office for only a few months when the Gulf War began. Everyone wondered how this new and comparatively young man would cope with such an awesome task. We heard daily reports on what was happening and he was seen visiting the troops in the Gulf. But by far the greatest moment of his career so far was when he addressed the nation. Speaking on television and looking directly at the cameras, he seemed to make instant eye contact with every individual watching. He explained in simple terms what had happened and why Britain was responding in the way it had. His manner made everyone watching feel that he was speaking directly to them.

Leading industrialists adopt the same manner when endeavouring to prove their point of view or to gain recognition for their company. Their whole attitude and confidence is maintained by the look in their eyes. They command authority not only in their voice, but also by staring directly at the people they wish to impress.

Besides eye contact, I am a constant observer of people's posture. It is the simplest of non-verbal clues. It has been noted that we tend to 'echo' one another's body posturing. Whenever we profoundly agree with one another, we seem to share the same posture. I know an individual who is a huge man. He is very well built and stands 6' 4" in his stockinged feet. His voice seems to complement his size, as it is low and with a very rich tone. His very presence therefore commands authority. He towers above almost everyone else and you can only imagine that his very thoughts, words and actions are supreme. You instinctively feel that his actual body size equals the size of his mind and that all he says must be correct. In actual fact, he is the mildest, sweetest-tempered person one could ever imagine. He is charming, but is not at all authoritarian and is open to suggestions from other people in almost any circumstances. The fact that he is big in size leads people to think that he also thinks big. They think that because of his size, he has an added advantage. He tells me that throughout his childhood everyone expected great things from him and it has been a burden to him all through life.

Similarly, small people are often dominated by the fact that they are small. They seem to have an underlying ambition because of their size to prove to everyone that they are as good, if not better than the majority. This is emphasised by the fact that many well-known and influential people are small. I was very surprised when I recently had the honour of meeting Her Majesty the Queen to see how petite she was and how beautiful her features were when she smiled. Many of the most notable personalities throughout history were also small, such as Nelson, Chopin and Hitler.

It is also important to note that a person's posture is a reflection of his former way of life. The way the shoulders are held, for example, can indicate an unhappy past or anger held in check. It has been observed that personal psychological dilemmas can become reinforced by your body structure. If someone has been through a prolonged period of depression and their body has sagged into a slump, their shoulders can literally become curved inward from the enormous weight of their burdens. The cause of such problems may eventually go away, but the habitual posture becomes a permanent fixture. It is entirely possible to get the body to reflect a secure, positive self-image once again, to restore the psyche that initiated the poor posture in the first place, but that would require conscious self-evaluation. After a prolonged period of time has passed, most women do not even realise the extent of their bad posture.

This brings to mind a wife who came to see me some time ago. She was a small, slight person in her mid-forties, who had brought up four children and who told me she was much happier running her home than attending lavish company functions. Unfortunately, her husband, having worked his way up from the 'shop floor', was now the managing director of a telecommunications company and expected her to be at his side on such occasions. As she sat opposite me, she seemed to show her obvious despair by her posture and general behaviour. Her shoulders were drooped, she would not make real eye contact and she constantly played with her fingers in a nervous movement. Her despair, it appears, was due to the fact that she was very unhappy with the current situation that she found herself in. Her husband seemed to her to be a totally different man from the one she had married. In the early days of their marriage, they had no money but worked together to provide a good home for their children. There seemed to be a purpose in everything they did. They were 'making it' together. Now her husband appeared to be in another world, working long and hard hours to maintain his position at the top of his company.

The most positive aspect was the fact that by coming to see us, she was indicating that she was ready to make a change. By making herself come to the office, she had made the first move to helping herself and to gaining some self-esteem. After a number of months, she began to gain a little more confidence within herself and she appeared to enjoy the role-play we use for gaining knowledge of small talk. Gradually, she became more and more interested in life, particularly when she could prove to herself that the techniques she had learnt really worked.

One day we were talking together and she confided that she always had a pain in her left shoulder. It was always there, but seemed to get progressively worse when she had to attend functions with her husband and his colleagues. I suggested that she might well be interested in learning about the Alexander Technique. This treatment is a specialised form of establishing if any permanent bone structure is incorrect or simply to discover if any pain caused is due to bad posture. The technician massages the area in question and demonstrates how you should sit, walk or stand. Many of our pains are due to bad posture it seems, and relief is given to many who use this special form of treatment.

We found details of the clinic nearest to where Patricia lived and we persuaded her to make the first appointment. She was told that her pain was due to intense nervous tension. Every time she was uptight about anything, she would tense her left shoulder muscles, causing a spasm each time. This in turn, made her droop her shoulders constantly. Eventually the treatment she received made her realise that by using the Alexander relaxation methods, she could overcome the spasms.

One day she appeared in the office and we could hardly believe our eyes! She was dressed in the most beautiful red suit with a black velvet half-collar. The jacket came right up to her neck so the line of black buttons was completely uninterrupted. Black accessories set it off superbly. But more significantly, she held herself high. Her shoulders were pulled back and she looked much taller than usual and extremely elegant. She had also obviously taken care over her make-up and hair. She looked and felt a totally different person. She had discovered, too, that by getting rid of the nagging pain she had endured for many years, she was not only able to stand much better, but she also felt so much better. She did not allow herself to become tense over her problems anymore and she began to open up to living. Feeling the way she did, she wanted new clothes to show off her new image. She began to watch her eating patterns, so that she would remain in good shape.

Most important, by making her posture correct again, after all the years she had spent bringing up her family, she found that she wanted to be seen with her husband. She was delighted to go to any company functions. She looked and felt so good, she wanted to share this with other people. Her husband was overjoyed.

Non-verbal communication is the yardstick against which words and emotions are measured. And you possess an advantage in this. Studies have shown that women are better than men at identifying an emotion portrayed non-verbally, are more sensitive to non-verbal communication through tones, and are superior to men in perceiving implications from dialogue. To be at such an advantage is to own a dominating spirit. Faces are the means by which we attempt to create an impression, and they will therefore be a major focus for displaying the impression of status, power, or authority. Language is intimately associated with, and supported by, your body's very own forms of communication. This reinforces the meaning of what you are saying. Although much is focused on the body overall, I believe that the face is the most crucial area to focus on when it comes to non-verbal clues.

The way expressions can be read from one's face can be broken down into three specific areas. First, you notice a person's personality traits. Your face is what people notice primarily. Hence, your facial expressions represent your personality, your overall characteristics. People have learned to control or manipulate, as some might say, their facial behaviour, so that others see only what the person wants them to see.

I ran across a girl who was very good at doing this. She was the assistant of a business acquaintance of mine and had worked with him for many years. He ran a successful recruitment agency and she would interview many of the applicants for jobs prior to their initial meeting with him. If a certain position had been advertised, she would also be the person who would interview the enthusiastic people who had applied for it, both before and after their interviews with her boss. Time and time again, I would see her talking through their applications with them and they would all try desperately to establish from her face whether she knew that they would be one of the lucky ones and get the job. Her face always remained a mask. She would be pleasant, of course, but she would not allow them to see whether they had the exact qualifications which were required or whether they were hopelessly misplaced. Either way, her face gave nothing away.

Later, I discovered she had gone through many personal problems when her husband had left her for another woman, but after several months had returned to her. I can honestly say, however, that whilst she was in her office, I saw no sign of the vast range of emotions she must have gone through during that time. She thought it professional to behave in this way, and indeed it was. But I used to wonder when *did* the mask fall, when did she break down and cry like the rest of us, or for that matter, when did she really laugh? Some people, like the girl in question, are determined that no matter what happens they will only let you see them in one particular way. I am sure they must be immensely strong-willed and disciplined but, personally, I warm much more to a person who shows their emotions sometimes. You can relate to them so much more, and often comparing one's hardships and joys can lead to new friendships.

But back to the issue of emotions . . . Facial expressions can signal interpersonal attitudes which are shown in an equally revealing manner. Vicky, for example, could manipulate her expression of emotion endlessly. Married to a very rich banker, she seemd to have everything money could buy: a large manor house in the country, a town flat, a Bentley as well as her own Porsche, plus a villa in Switzerland and a boat in the West Indies. She was a super girl and was the only child of a couple who had brought her into the world when they were in their mid-forties. Consequently, she always had her own way with them and when she married her husband, twenty-five years her senior, we all knew she would still continue to do so. Whenever she didn't get her own way, she would start the tears immediately. We have all seen it happen with other girls, haven't we? As soon as they think that things are not going to happen in the way they wish, or they can't have something they want, they begin the waterworks!

However, where she differed from other girls was the way in which she could produce the tears on other occasions, which made people warm to her as they felt she cared so much. For example, one of her husband's employees died suddenly of a heart attack. He had worked for her husband for many years and of course his death was a blow to everyone, especially to his wife and children. Vicky hardly knew him. She had met him only on a couple of occasions at a company dinner and once when she had visited her husband's office. She and her husband attended the funeral and Vicky stood in the church with the rest of his family, with tears streaming down her face. Her husband and his colleagues, together with some of the family, were amazed. How caring she seemed, how distressed she looked. But it was all an act! As soon as she got back into the car to take them both home, she looked at her husband and said, 'Well darling, how did I do?'

In the same way, she would be able to make herself laugh when she thought it right to do so. On one occasion, I remember seeing her at a cocktail party, apparently enjoying herself enormously with one of her husband's partners. She was smiling at his words and she would toss her head back and laugh out loud for all to see that she was in good company. The man she was with showed his pleasure at the obvious interest Vicky was showing in what he had to say. When I visited the ladies' room she joined me. 'God, what a bore!' she said. 'I thought you were enjoying yourself,' I replied. It was only then that she told me she had developed this facade for all corporate occasions. 'Max tells me how I should behave and to whom, and in return he buys me what I want,' she said. 'It is a very good arrangement!'

Perhaps this is carrying simulated emotion a little too far, but as long as people are not hurt by it and enjoy being on the receiving end of Vicky's dramatics without realising it has been stage managed, then surely there is no harm in it. People like to see response and animation from colleagues, friends and loved ones alike, and it tends to make them want your company more.

Finally, interaction signals and movements associated with speech can be expressed by rather swift movements of parts of the face. For example, eyebrow raising, wide eye opening, squinting, dropping your lower jaw and the like.

On occasions, I would come into contact with a real bore of a conversationalist but found that facial expressions made him really react! He was one of those people who loved his job so much he would never stop talking about it. He was a company 'doctor' and would be called in when a company was in trouble and endeavour to plan and implement systems to make it profitable again. He had the unfortunate knack of beginning to tell you a story about a firm and then digressing from the main thread to tell you other unimportant details which were totally irrelevant to the main storyline. Every single detail had to be carefully explained at length until you, the listener, were totally lost as to what he was trying to say. The point of his story was gone! This happened time and time again with me as he was on the same charity committee as myself and would make a habit of always sitting next to me at the meetings.

As you now know, I suggest that one should encourage people to talk about themselves so that you can, in turn, 'switch off' if required. This man needed no such encouragement. Far from it! He would go on and on, interspersed with saying, 'I seem to be doing all the talking to-day!' It was only after I had spent quite a few such days with him that I discovered if I simply raised my eyebrows at some point or when he took a breath, he would stop and lose his concentration. Without saying a word, my facial movement seemed to distract him. I started doing this more and more and he appeared to slow up in his conversation with me. One afternoon he explained that he would not talk so much on this occasion, as I had indicated to him that I was questioning his views. He interpreted my raising my eyebrows in this way as doubting what he was describing but it had the desired effect.

One of the wives on my course had a habit of stopping bores by screwing her face up as if she were in pain. They would stop talking immediately and ask what the trouble was. When asked this question, she would simply shrug and say, 'Oh, it's nothing really' and change the subject. We must all be able to tell how people experience emotions. We must be alert to what someone's face is telling us about their feelings and whether these feelings are genuine or meant to deceive. You can't rely solely on another person's words, for at times, even *he* isn't sure about his feelings regarding the issue under discussion. Let's take the case of the barrister. He can't necessarily trust the spoken words of his witness, or client. He requires additional information, like that which someone's face can give him, to let him know what really lies underneath.

How often do you feel an intuition or hunch about someone you meet? You may not be aware of it, but it is usually a facial expression that caused such an impression upon you. You may only experience something intangible about the person without being able consciously to trace the source of your impression. Facial behaviour can be controlled or uncontrolled. Someone can be expressive entirely deliberately, while someone else reveals their feelings without intending to. Some are honest, while others stretch the limits of the truth at every opportunity. The wife of a prominent politician once said to me that her husband was so used to manipulating other people that he would even lie as to what he ate for breakfast. The dilemma for you is to distinguish what is genuine.

Imagine that someone receives distressing news. If there is an expression of defeat on his face, it would have occurred natur- ally. He did not think how to 'arrange' his facial expression. But then his expression shifts to anger and aggression. He has made a deliberate and self-conscious shift in facial muscles. He wants you to think of him in another way. His facial behaviour was modified to express only slight concern, when in reality he is experiencing a major blow.

This was never more so than in the recent case of Margaret Thatcher. We all remember well seeing her coming down the steps of the British Embassy in Paris in October 1990 and facing the world press. While she had been carrying out her duties in Paris, her fellow politicians had been lining up against her. She knew by then that she would not be able to call upon many of her so-called friends to assist her and vote for her to remain prime minister. It must have been a bombshell for her. Similar parlia- mentary votes had taken place before and she always won hands down. This time, however, it was different. She knew by then that things were tough and that they would get tougher. But nothing of this showed on her face that day. She faced the cameras and told the country, 'I will fight and fight to win!' As history will tell, she did not fight. When she returned to her country, which she was busily defending in Paris against other countries' heads of state, she realised that her political friends as well as opponents wanted a change. After ten years, they were looking for a new prime minister.

Many of us felt very sorry for her as she left Number 10 Downing Street for the last time. As she turned to look back at the place which had been her home for so long, the place where she had made monumental decisions on our behalf and where she had entertained everyone, from President Bush to the young Scout of the year, we noticed her eyes fill with tears. She again faced the world's cameras and spoke of her delight in John Major's achievement and wished him well before setting off to Buckingham Palace to officially hand her resignation to the Queen. No one, with the possible exception of her husband, Dennis, will ever know how she really felt. One can only imagine the anguish and loneliness she must have experienced as, prior to her resignation, she interviewed each one of her cabinet ministers to establish what they thought she should do. Almost all said she should resign for the sake of the party.

Her facial expressions showed none of her profound emotions. Throughout it all, she remained outwardly calm and smiling as she waved at the crowds of well-wishers. Her enemies and friends agreed upon one thing: she was a true professional!

At other times, people have the ability to give the impression that they are experiencing an emotion when they feel nothing at all. An individual may portray an emotion that appears to be sorrow or joy when actually he doesn't feel anything, or else feels disappointment or envy. You need to control facial expression, because being an executive wife is your vocation. It requires that you portray that which will enhance your husband's career goals and professional image. If you are the wife of a diplomat, for instance, then the job requires that you show no facial expression at all. You are constantly neutral, allowing those who come into contact with you to see you as an unbiased, competent individual. You must control your facial behaviour because it is to your advantage to do so.

So how can you distinguish a genuine facial expression of emotion from a false one that is intended to mislead you? The answer is, you can't – most of the time. You can only learn to judge people by their other actions as well as by their expressions of emotion.

Take Vicky for example. By deliberately exhibiting emotion which is false, she leaves herself open to criticism that she does not carry her expressions through in practice. It would have been far better for her not to have cried at the funeral, but to write to the wife of her husband's employee saying how sorry she was to hear of his death. Equally, by attempting to laugh outrageously at every one of her companion's jokes, she was in danger of being found out by overdoing the laughter. More experienced people can see that inevitably her mask is going to fall. How much better it would be if she made herself genuinely interested in her friends so that her expressions were spontaneous and much more effective.

Most people rightly rely on facial behaviour as being more trustworthy than the spoken word. You have known many times when someone was trying to deceive you by the look on their face. We have all been taken in by facial expressions more often than we care to acknowledge. The ways in which we present ourselves non-verbally not only conveys the norms of our society, but they are our personal signature above all. It is an important means by which to express to society our worthiness or lack of it. A signal regarding appearances is a message not only concerning the person, but about what they are saying. An ambitious business presentation spoken by a knowledgeable individual with bored eyes, a withdrawn face, and a sagging body would not appeal much to an audience. He is conveying through his body that he really should be ignored because how could anything important or amusing come out of such a careless-looking person?

Remember the famous Kennedy–Nixon television debate in 1960? The contrast between Kennedy's vitality and enthusiasm and Nixon's fatigue (in addition to his stony nature) was seen as more important than anything either man had to say.

8

How to maintain executive style

Being a corporate wife is wonderful! It can be exciting, alluring, glamorous, challenging, unconventional or powerful. The choices are yours and yours alone. You can revel in your position and be exhilarated with all the options of being married to the great one. These options are not limited by your educational and social background, by the number of years you have been married, by your ideas or goals. They are limited solely by the boundaries of your imagination and the strength of your character.

However, we do live in a visual society which projects a narrow view of the 'ideal', thus making it necessary for you to adapt to that which is considered the appropriate corporate image. You don't have to be tall, thin and beautiful, but you should be clever, well-groomed and impeccably dressed. If you don't fit the desired mould, you become unacceptable and feel inadequate and undeserving. You should not be constantly searching to find an image through needless expenditure and sacrifice. It isn't necessary to suffer deprivations. Instead, simply learn the acceptable limits of appropriate appearance and then imprint your own personal style onto it.

Here, we are about to focus on you, the corporate wife, whether you are twenty or fifty years of age. If you are fighting the urge to come along, trying to convince yourself that the inside of a person is far more valuable than any 'image', rest assured that I do not disagree with you. Making yourself externally appealing is a complete waste of time if all you desire is to become a beautiful shell. However, I believe that a complete being is an alignment of one's inner beauty and outer appeal. The two can be so finely interwoven that they are inseparable. Being truly marvellous and competent on the inside, while neglecting the outside, is like having invented the world's most magnificent product and never putting it on the market. If no one knows about it, it won't be in demand.

Some years ago I attended a political reception held in the magnificent building just behind Pall Mall where the Foreign Secretary officially entertains heads of state. The beautiful oak staircase faces you as you enter the main entrance hall, and leads up to the main reception room on the first floor. Ivory silk wallpaper complements the pale colours of the soft furnishings, together with the dark wood of the antique furniture. In the main room I counted four crystal chandeliers, and at one end of the room french windows opened out to a patio overlooking St James's Park on one side and Pall Mall on the other.

It was my first visit to this mansion and I was very excited about it. The occasion was to entertain the various European ministers who were visiting London for a conference. I took some time to consider what I would wear and decided on a short, royal blue, silk dress with high-heeled black shoes and my small padded black Chanel bag to slip over my shoulder. I found myself wondering what others would wear. After all, most of the women attending would be wives of politicians. After I had been introduced to my host and talked to a few other people, I stood and looked at the other guests who were standing around the room. I really could not believe what I was seeing! The majority of women were wearing dowdy, old-fashioned dresses and suits. So many of them looked as though they had not taken any trouble at all; not only that, as if they hadn't changed their hairstyles in years. Many of the ladies wore little or no make-up.

Now I know I shall get a lot of 'flak' by implying that wives of politicians are dowdy and do not care about their appearance. This of course is not true. I know plenty who would leave the rest of us standing with their elegant dressing and up-to-date hairstyles. At the annual political conferences, for example, you will see many ladies who are extremely attractive and take very great care over their clothes, and use these occasions to emphasise that fact. All I can say is, that on that particular evening, this was certainly not the case. It seemed such a pity that, for various reasons, the ladies attending did not appear to bother too much about how they looked. Maybe it was because they have to attend so many similar receptions that they have become bored.

One of the main problems executive and political wives suffer from today is a lack of basic self-esteem. After all, unless you are a high achiever yourself, you may feel that you are merely married to success and have not earned the right to feel responsible for any of it yourself. This is especially true among new wives or those who have stayed home for twenty years raising children while their husbands were 'out in the world'. But, of course, you are an important part of his success and as such must appreciate yourself for it. Truly feeling proud or liking yourself in this regard is not a sin or a punishable crime. It is required of you! It is also required of you to look the part. Why, this was even true in biblical times. Remember Esther? She spent an entire year of her life just experimenting with perfumes, ointments, and fashions to become as attractive as possible. Frivolous, you say? She became queen of her land and eventually she was responsible for saving the Jewish population from extinction. Her appearance, her image was not in vain. She had a mission! And, so do you. Perhaps not as grand, but it could mean attracting or maintaining a certain clientele that is crucial to your husband's business successes. You probably won't have to go as far as Esther, but your dedication to appearance and self-improvement will undoubtedly help you attain a certain status.

The editor of a prestigious British newspaper has a wife who is famous as the long-legged beauty in the soap opera *Dallas*. Although she was born in Texas, she has lived so long in England that she was recently cast as JR's English wife. Nevertheless, Gayle Hunnicutt is a real Southern Belle. Her upbringing in the States made her aware that to look good was all-important. As a result she is now extremely elegant, has perfect manners and is well respected for being a superb hostess. She unashamedly spends time on her appearance with make-up experts, acupuncture and occasional visits to health farms. Even though perhaps some would say she has an added incentive because she still remains an actress, she ensures that she looks equally attractive in the country at the weekends or entertaining in London.

Tina Brown is the wife of the former editor of *The Times*, Harold Evans. She always appears glamorous on every occasion and spends time selecting her clothes to show her own style. Maybe the fact that she herself is the editor of *Vanity Fair* has got something to do with it. Her father was the film producer, George Brown, and she was brought up to want a glittering life and achieved it early. Her beautiful blonde hair and vivid blue eyes complement her clothes sense. Although she was born with many advantages, she too works on her appearance and ensures she keeps fit in spite of her very busy schedules and constant flights from New York to London.

There is absolutely no denying that people treat us differently when we look professional. Looking good is important. No matter what your means and status, you have experienced the influence of this difference on many occasions. If you are not impressed with the powerful-looking, well-dressed woman when you see her, you are not being honest with yourself. We automatically conjure up an entire image of what her life must be like. If it didn't hold any enviable qualities, let's just say that we wouldn't be speculating at all. She demands special attention; better treatment is simply expected. An embarrassed-looking, shy, introverted person probably does not feel comfortable being in the same vicinity with her, let alone expect equal treatment. Clothing deprivation has a significant relationship to a lack of social confidence and to low self-concepts.

I have a bright Chanel jacket which I wear at some of our courses. Underneath it I wear a plain black dress. When we are discussing clothes with impact, I ask the wives to consider what I am wearing. I demonstrate that by wearing my red jacket, I look and feel more confident, more professional. They understand that if I entered a room with lots of people, I would probably stand out with my long hair and red jacket. Take the jacket away, however, and I would dissolve into the background.

Clothes can do so much for us. They can make us feel good about ourselves. Wearing bright colours, even if it is only a brightly coloured scarf tucked underneath your chin, can do wonders for your confidence. It is no concidence that many of the top professional women wear bright reds, blue, green, vivid pinks and yellow. One identifies a strong colour with a strong woman. At a women's conference I attended recently, these vivid colours featured very much within the audience.

The colours we wear often reflect our mood of the moment. Sometimes we want to wear dark blacks and browns – we are happy to be in the background. When next you are feeling low or worried about something, note what you are wearing on those bad days. Subconsciously, you will go for the greys and the dark colours. Similarly, when life is good, you will want to go for something much lighter. Taking the trouble to wear one of the bright colours which suit you best, coupled with clothes which have a good, clean cut to them, where the hem rests just at the right length to suit your particular shaped legs, complemented by matching accessories, means *impact*. You will find that people will respond to you in quite a different manner. Whatever you aim to do, people will consider you to be confident and professional. Your efforts will be worth it.

During the Middle Ages, one's position or status was easily identifiable and thus the accompanying privileges were unquestionably granted. In such times, many societies also passed decrees known as Sumptuary Laws to forbid the wearing of specific fashions by certain members of society. But as class barriers weakened and wealth could be more easily and rapidly converted into gentility, the system which dictated those distinctions became outdated. The overthrow of the rules was then replaced by a display of wealth: finest fabrics, exceptional tailoring and exclusive styles.

No one would certainly go to all this trouble if the symbols of one's presence were merely frivolous, superficial and basically not important. One of the basic laws of human nature is that most people judge others by first impression, and that includes their clothing. They respond accordingly. Rank and one's opinion of oneself are indicated by costume. It isn't difficult to distinguish an executive from the secretary, a student from the professor, a doctor from his associate, even during his off-duty hours and while not in 'uniform'.

One of the girls who is part of our team has a system she practises often which supports this reasoning. Alison is responsible for training wives for job interviews. Some wives, once they use our programme, often want to go out and get a job. Alison ensures that they are given interview skills so that they can go to these with confidence. However, she also is requested by some important companies to do some specialised sales training. Selling luxury yachts, leather goods, prestige cars, expensive jewellery, for example, requires a very special type of persuasion. Not for these do you require the hard sell. Alison therefore trains staff to develop skills to build up business relationships and to provide the ultimate service. However, before she sets up her first training session, she will go into the store or showroom dressed in old jeans, a sweatshirt and leather jacket, and ask to be sold what they have to sell. A few days later, she will go back to the same place dressed in a designer suit, with expensive accessories. She maintains that on her first visit she is met with disdain, lack of interest and sometimes rudeness, while on the second visit nothing is too much trouble for them to provide her with a good service.

Imagine their surprise when she tells them on their first morning at the session what she has done. Perhaps the first lesson that they learn from her is that although someone is poorly dressed, it does not necessarily mean they have to be treated differently. In the case of these luxury items, it is not always the well-dressed person who has the money to purchase them, even though they may look as though they have. It is only human nature to assume that if one's appearance is casual, one will not have any money, when the opposite might be the case.

In earlier times as well as today, it was perhaps considered foolishly extravagant and deliberately deceptive by some to dress beyond one's position and means. But you have often heard it said, and I strongly agree, that you should not dress for the position you are in, but for the position you desire to obtain. Always remember that status in relation to clothing is very much alive and well.

But let's look at the issue from another point of view. A guide to good manners written only fifty years ago explains that: 'An honest heart may beat beneath the ragged coat, a brilliant intellect may rise above the bright checked suit and the yellow tie, the man in the shabby suit may be a famous writer, a girl in the untidy blouse may be an artist of great promise, but as a general rule, the chances are against it, as such people are dull, flat, stale and unprofitable both to themselves and to other people.'

Can virtue ever shine through an undesirable appearance? Not in Cinderella's case. She could not have been seen as an attractive and able being underneath the rags and the mop of hair. The attainment of fine clothes, however, enhanced her true personal grace. So many Cinderellas today are diamonds in the rough. They are corporate wives in outdated dresses or cheap, shoddy outfits. A woman cannot feel confident and good about herself if she feels she doesn't fit into the business social atmosphere. Her true potential is rarely fully realised under such circumstances.

Very often you discover that people see you in quite another way from the way in which you see yourself. You face yourself each morning in the mirror and prepare for the day ahead. Throughout that day, you have a mental image of yourself and how you think you look to others. Sometimes, however, you are pulled up sharply at remarks which are made to you by others who obviously see you quite differently. Let's take one morning when, from the first moment you open your eyes, you wish you could stay in bed all day and not face the world. You have had a bad night perhaps, or you have worked extra hard on a project or have had visitors who outstayed their welcome. You feel jaded and slow. You look into the bathroom mirror and know that you have some work to do on yourself in order to face the day. This mood might be with you all day, but it can suddenly change when someone unexpectedly says, 'Hello! you're looking very attractive today! I love the colour of your blouse. It suits your hair colouring very well.' All of a sudden you feel much better, the world seems a brighter place. Similarly, you know how good it is for your morale when a friend says that someone you have met recently told her how attractive they think you are. You automatically feel much better about yourself. Your smile gets bigger – you begin to have a warm feeling inside, knowing that someone has noticed the real you.

On some occasions, unfortunately, the reverse can happen. I know a super lady who is very attractive to look at. She always looks immaculate. You never see her nail varnish chipped and although she tells me she has her hair tinted, you never see any hint of black roots. She makes sure that her weight keeps much the same throughout the year and her clothes are chosen with equal care. Perfection! She told me one day, however, that she had not always been meticulous about her appearance. She had married young and had three small babies very quickly, one after another. Obviously she was kept very busy looking after them as well as doing the household chores. Her husband was a stockbroker and they would have to entertain quite often and were invited to a number of events. On these occasions, she would take care over herself and try to keep in fashion. She liked to sew, and for formal events would often make her own long dresses. But, for the most part, she didn't feel she had enough time to trouble too much about her appearance. (I think all of us who have had to cope with small children know that feeling well.)

One Christmas she eagerly opened all her presents – from her husband, from her mother, and from her mother-in-law. From her husband, she received a microwave (all right, she did say to him that she wanted one!); from her mother, talcum powder from a well-known chemist and some gloves; while from her mother-in-law she received a bottle of lavender water! It was this final present which made my friend pull herself up with a jolt! It was not the value of the presents she resented, but it was the contents which upset her so much. A microwave oven, gloves and old ladies' lavender water, when she longed for exotic perfume, exciting lingerie and lots of junk jewellery! Why did her own family not know that she was screaming inside to be seen as someone quite different from how they obviously saw her?

The next day, she was alone in the house and stood in front of a full-size mirror and, with her notepad beside her, she wrote down all her bad points as well as the good ones. On the plus side, she had nice eyes, her complexion was good. She had a small, but well-rounded, bust and slim arms. Oh, and her teeth looked nice when she smiled. On the bad side, her hair was a dull brown colour, her hips and thighs too big, and her nails were slightly bitten.

Once she had made herself do this exercise, she knew what she had to do. First, she went to her local hairdresser and asked advice on her hair. After much discussion, it was decided to tint her hair a beautiful, rich auburn colour. When she looked at herself for the first time with the new colour, she was surprised to see that the colour had made her complexion look more pale, almost opaque, and the small laughter lines around her eyes were almost gone. Next, she visited the beauty counter at a nearby store and was given advice on good skin care, as well as new make-up with slightly different colours from those she had always used before, because of her new hair colouring. Finally, she joined a local health club and sought help on dealing with her slight overweight. She was shown how to use the special equipment for breaking down her fat by doing lots of exercise. During the first month, she noticed that already her skirts and trousers fitted much more easily over her hips and, with a healthy diet, she was able to come down a complete dress size in three months as she had lost so much weight. Her nails took a little longer to grow, but with all the healthy food she was now eating, they were at last beginning to look more elegant. As soon as she could, she painted them with a clear nail varnish so as to discourage her from biting them.

From the moment of her realisation that people saw her quite differently from how she imagined herself to be, she never looked back. Her beauty régime is of paramount importance to her now.

Fashion is a necessary 'prop' in establishing and maintaining the treatment and position in the business environment that you desire. The clothes you choose to wear contribute to the stabilisation of your projected image. They can even frequently be considered more important than your posture, speech, intellect or facial expression, when the first and brief impression is the only opportunity you have. Appearance is possibly even more important than language in communicating an impression of yourself to others. The initial impression you create will most likely be a crucial one. As in the theory that fine feathers make fine birds, first impressions are largely derived from outward appearances and established by non-verbal cues and thus it would be most difficult and quite risky to ignore them. The application of good fashion sense certainly boosts your morale and confidence level. It is a significant force in the enhancement of yourself. Where fashion sense is used positively, it contributes to your feelings of self-acceptance and self-esteem. It is no accident, for instance, that black leaders are among the best dressed politicians and athletes in the United States. Jesse Jackson may live in a modest, middle-class neighbourhood, but his shirts and suits are bought in Manhattan's exclusive Bijan, where corporate heads and international heads of state shop by appointment only. They have an image to protect. *You* have an image to protect. That is why it is necessary to give it the full attention it deserves.

Louise Hay in her very popular book *You Can Heal Your Life* advocates that when we really love ourselves, everything in our life works. She emphasises that if we tell ourselves constantly that we approve of ourselves, it is a powerful base to ensure that our beauty will come from within. We all know that some people we meet in our daily lives have 'inner' beauty. No matter what they wear, they offer freedom of spirit, their smile is welcoming and warm, and they are seen to be attractive by everyone. Louise Hay asks in her book for us to make an affirmation each day, by looking into a mirror, looking at ourselves directly in the eyes and saying 'I am really beautiful'. At first it is very hard to do, but if you continue to do this every day, no matter how silly it sounds, it really does work. You will suddenly feel beautiful and you will discover an inner strength which confirms what you have always known – that your own special beauty is there, it just sometimes needs to be encouraged a little.

My mother always told me that we owe it to other people to look our best. 'How much better it is to talk to people who take pride in their appearance,' she used to say. 'It adds a sparkle to the conversation.' She sent me to a convent school where we were taught at a very young age to always try to look our best. 'They teach you to grow up like a lady,' my mother explained. I am not suggesting for one moment that no one will take any notice of you unless you are well dressed. Of course, that would be nonsense. Equally, I am not saying that people will respect you more if, although you are very well dressed with immaculate make-up and hair, you talk a load of nonsense. But to take pride in ourselves adds to our self-esteem and makes others respect us and want to be associated with us.

A quick glance at a corporate wife's appearance can give a wealth of information about her character, her husband's level of success, their status in life. As one psychologist in the late 1930s stated:

'With briefest visual perception, a complex mental process is aroused, resulting within a very short time, 30 seconds or less, in judgement of the sex, age, size, nationality, profession and social caste of the person, together with some estimate of his temperament, his ascendance, friendliness, neatness, and even his trustworthiness and integrity. With no further acquaintance many impressions are erroneously formed. They show the swift totalizing nature of our judgements.'

When the wife of an executive or political figure is seen carelessly or unsuitably attired, those observing her immediately assume that she has little concern for personal appearance and limited regard for the opinions of others. They are further even guilty of extending this appraisal so that the woman is assumed to be unfriendly or even rude.

Having previously made some unfavourable comments about politicians' wives, I would like to take this opportunity to redress this by giving an example of how clothes can influence a husband's career.

Let us take the example of the competition which ensued between Michael Heseltine, Douglas Hurd and of course John Major. The journalists from all the national newspapers went overboard to interview the wives and to criticise their appearances. Mrs Hurd was seen mostly wearing brogues and tweeds in a country setting with her small children. She looked extremely attractive and just right for her setting. Michael Heseltine's wife was constantly seen in the press, always wearing just the right outfit for any occasion. When her husband and her two daughters and son were pictured with her at their country house, she looked youthful and fashionable in well-cut jeans and jumper. Her hair was cut so cleverly that even when the wind took it during their photo session, it bounced back into shape immediately. Photographed outside her London town house with her husband whilst he was being interviewed prior to the last count of the last vote, she looked serene and calm in a black dress with the patent belt showing off her slim waist. The journalists ran out of suitable ways to describe her appearance and obvious dress sense.

When finally the vote was known and John Major became one of the youngest prime ministers we have had in this country, his wife meanwhile could not have been prepared for the enormous barrage of criticism she received from the press regarding her appearance. She has her own style and is happy with it, but because she wore the same blue suit for two days after her husband's election, with full skirt and short jacket, she was 'pounded' by the press both national and international. Later she was seen entertaining at No 10 wearing a beautiful peach-coloured suit which complemented her own colouring. The press immediately said that the image makers had got to her. But in fact she has made it clear to everyone that she will not be told what to wear; not for her the image makers who would change her style. She has to be admired for her strength in resisting all attempts to persuade her otherwise. She has indicated to the country, 'This is the way I am and this is how I will stay!'

The above example, however, indicates how people react to the way we dress and how our appearance can influence others particularly in the case of political spouses. Look at the case of John Kennedy and his wife Jackie Onassis. Many Americans have said that he got to be president because he had personality and she had style. The power of appearance and identification is well portrayed, however humorously, in a recent *New Yorker* magazine cartoon. The sketch shows two judges and one says to the other: 'This daily metamorphosis never fails to amaze me. Around the house, I'm a perfect idiot. I come to court, put on a black robe and, by God, I'm it!'

For the corporate wife, the aura of confidence, a blend of inner confidence and outer polish is the goal.

9

How to use colour to enhance your image

Many an executive wife has opted for the safe 'neutral' colour when faced with decisions to make on which outfit to wear, which table setting to consider, the type of flowers to send and the like. Much confusion can be eliminated and terrific strides can be made when you stop and consider all the options you have with the uses of colours.

Colour is always with us. Like other tremendous forces, it has the ability to enhance or destroy. Hence, it becomes a necessity to learn to employ the powers of colour to our own advantage. Woven into today's society in such an extensive manner as to be an integral part of it, colour is often taken for granted, but we must not ignore it. In fact, so many people have experienced the profound and emotional impact of colour, that they attribute to it powers that perhaps are more suited to a person's psyche. Mystics tend to assign virtues to the spectrum while scientists, of course, are suspicious of anything connected with the emotions. You may already be aware, for instance, that great English poets have made reference to colour extensively in their writing. The extent of Pope's use of colour, for example, was quite significant: he used it more than Coleridge, Byron or Keats, twice as much as Chaucer or Milton and two and a half times more than Shakespeare.

Continued familiarity with colour has frequently aroused and stimulated thought and speculation concerning its influence over us. Hasn't it always been a key aim of the artist to discover the powers of colours and to employ their powers of suggestion in his appeals to man's emotions? Everyone experiences the genuine pleasure of a dramatic sunset or deep blue ocean. It is awesome to see it before our eyes. However, *seeing* anything requires more than just observing it point-blank. Such perception is a complex mental process of which we are rarely aware. There is so much to understand about the way colour affects our moods, energy levels, perception of other people and places. Goethe wrote that 'People experience a great delight in colour generally. The eye requires it as much as it does light.' To him, yellow was bright and possessed a 'serene, gay, softly exciting character.' Red had the most energy. 'It is not to be wondered at that impetuous, robust, uneducated man, should be especially pleased with this colour,' he wrote. 'Among savage nations the inclination for it has been universally remarked.' Blue, to him, was cold, gloomy and melancholy; violet or purple were disquieting. 'It may be safely assumed that a garment of a perfectly deep blue-red would be intolerable,' he claimed. Green was calm and quiescent. 'The beholder has neither the wish nor the power to imagine a state beyond it.'

It is obvious to most of us that colour has been displayed by nature lavishly, purposefully and effectively. We have adapted its use to our purposes quite well in addition, but with advances in science and psychology we find that colour can be a valuable assistant in the performance of our numerous tasks and duties. Colour is such a monumental natural force that it should be an indispensable part of our everyday life in general, but specifically when you have a goal, no opportunity to win the upper hand should be overlooked. It has such a power to influence people's actions that it can work every day either to your benefit or disadvantage. So why not allow it to be instrumental in diminishing your unprofitable qualities and let it help you to magnify the better ones?

Realising the importance of colour as it pertains to the clothes one wears and the colours we surround ourselves with everyday, I turned to a leading authority in the field of colour physchology, Megan Windsor-Williams, who is the founder of the Study of Color Psychology in Beverly Hills, California. While I was visiting Ms Windsor-Williams, she shared some ideas which make up her philosophy. It is important to remember that every day you are making choices based on how you perceive yourself or how you feel others perceive you. Get rid of the cobwebs that have tied you to your past choices and emerge as a butterfly from its chrysalis. Colour is the most powerful factor you can use, she claims. Every woman wants to bring her beauty to the forefront by using the colours which come from within and are a part of herself – her own 'colour signature.' Ms Windsor-Williams goes on to observe that the pattern or harmonies formed in each individual are as varied as the rainbow, which may appear to be almost any shading of colours depending on the time of day and the size of the raindrops.

If you are wearing colours that are in harmony with you and clothing designs that show you off best, you will feel secure about your appearance and free to be yourself! When you, as the executive wife, feel good about yourself, it gives you the freedom to enjoy, assist or gain favours from others.

While no two individuals are exactly alike, certain characteristics – physical, emotional and social – seem to typify the individual with certain colour groupings. We have placed the individuals of like colouring into four groups which we identify with the four seasons found in nature. To create a harmonious whole, you must also consider the lines of your garments, the fabrics they are made from and the accessories you choose as well. Let's begin by exploring the creation of a harmonious whole by using your colours, the lines of your garments, the fabrics they are made from and the appropriate accessories for you.

While I was conducting a seminar in San Francisco several years ago, I met Kateland. She is a beautiful, tall, willowy woman with medium blonde hair, peaches-and-cream complexion and bright blue eyes. Her husband is one of the leading law enforcement officers in the pretty town of Twin Peaks located in the mountains of Southern California. When you drive up to their home, it reflects the buoyancy and freedom expressed in persons of Spring colouring. The house is in a countryside setting with a garden full of brightly coloured flowers of yellow, red, pink, blue and lavender. The back of the house is all glass with a view over Southern California where on a clear day you can see to the Catalina Islands in the Pacific Ocean.

She has three beautiful, lively children who play all round her and never distract her from the chores at hand. Kateland makes life a playground for her children, always instilling virtues in a delightful atmosphere. During the spring, summer and autumn months, Kateland models for publications and fashion shows. She also teaches at a nationally acclaimed modelling and finishing school. But in the winter, she hits the ski slopes located close to her house while teaching other 'would be's' how to ski. She remarked, 'I just live for the days I can be out skiing and teaching.' But with all the attention that has been focused on her by others, she was at a loss as what to do when it came to putting herself together for her husband's social business-related functions. I knew who could help!

Before we talk about solving Kateland's problems, I wish to mention Judy. Judy is a buoyant, petite, blonde, green-eyed woman with unbounded energy. Everyone is drawn to Judy. She lives on an island which is adjacent to one of the Southern California states. The island is made up of grand homes, golf courses, horse trails and jogging paths. She is married to a real estate tycoon who has an ongoing need for his wife to be beside him to assist in entertaining his clients and business associates who come from far and near. I met Judy while we were developing a resort. She, too, heads up her own business as a convention planner for people in the entertainment field. Her conventions draw the glamorous owners of modelling and talent agencies seeking fresh faces and talent. She never has a dull day and can carry on a telephone conversation while directing her staff on projects at hand. She thrives on being surrounded by people – lots of people carrying out highly energetic projects.

Her style was vibrant and creative, which suited her profession well, but it was too often misplaced or simply 'wrong' when dealing with her husband's mainly conservative and mature clientele. After Judy had her colour profile developed and her wardrobe planned, she used these tools religiously. Being involved in her husband's work as well, Judy says she now always wears a special suit the colour of her eyes, which makes her come across as highly credible when negotiating any contracts. In Judy's words, 'At first I was sceptical about the use of my eye colour giving me a high degree of credibility. But now I know it works! Every time!' However, soon enough, we'll have to get Judy to wear a different suit . . .

Kateland and Judy and others whose colouring is light and bright have a cheerful, spontaneous anticipation of life. Their energy seems boundless and their body motions are quick. The individuals of spring are perennially youthful; they love people and for them it is fun just to have them drop in. Kateland and Judy take a lively interest in many projects, love parades, picnics and balls. They enjoy sports and the outdoors, flowers and gardens. All women of Spring colouring should strive for a feeling of animation and activity in the lines and design of their clothing. They can be chic wearing ruffled or gathered lines like those of the daffodil, particularly round their necks. They can wear a bunch of flowers on their suit, coat or hat. The fabrics best suited to the woman of Spring colouring are sheer, crisp and bouncy with a smooth, fragile texture. They also wear broderie anglaise and voile. And yes, blue jeans! If they wear floral designs, they should select open-faced flowers such as daisies. Also good are bird and butterfly designs: designs which express animation. Polka dots and ginghams are made for the Spring woman as well.

Kateland and Judy wear clear, vibrant colours now to express the animation and cheerfulness that characterises the woman of Spring. The colours they wear well include cherry, coral, apricot, daffodil, grapefruit, buttercup, apple, new leaf green, blueberry, cornflower, violet and lilac. Their jewellery is tinkling, airy, and delicate filigree in pale yellow gold. The precious stones they use include aquamarine, corals, yellow sapphire and diamonds. The Spring woman should achieve a fresh, airy feeling in her fragrances. The light scents of flowers, fern and grasses are for her.

While on a mission on behalf of a client with the United Nations, I had the pleasure of meeting Margaret. She is a woman of soft, elegant colouring – light brown hair, delicate skin and grey-violet eyes. She thrives on keeping a well-ordered home. Her husband is a colonel in the United States Army with a position demanding a lot of diplomatic entertaining of visiting dignitaries from the United Nations, NATO and many foreign countries as well as from the military community. She is a fabulous support for her husband's chosen career. She loves gourmet cooking and is one of the most creative entertainers among the military wives. Everyone lines up to be on her guest list! Margaret is very musical also. She is an accomplished artist on the piano and organ. She always has handwork such as crewel embroidery or needlepoint close by. She told me that when she is wearing her American Beauty Rose red, everyone tells her how feminine she appears; when she is wearing her cream skin colour everyone compliments her on how beautiful she looks (since the basic skin tone when worn frames the face and places the features in the forefront).

I also recall the story of a beautiful, petite Japanese lady I met while in Tokyo. Mimi was a newly married woman whose husband was the fourth generation head of a family-owned import/export business. Mimi was sent to have her colours analysed and for a wardrobe consultation. Like everyone exposed to the field of colour analysis, she was under the mistaken impression that everyone of oriental descent was in the 'Winter' classification – all one colour. Much to her surprise and pleasure, she had a beautiful violet undertone to her skin and the colours which came from within placed her in a 'Summer' category. Her colour profile contains colours of milky white touched with violet for her skin tone, a pale gold which reflects the colour shining from her eyes, and then the rest of the jewel-like colours which show off her natural beauty.

Mimi's husband, Tiho, decided to have his colours analysed at her urging and he turned out to be the Spring classification. Mimi and her husband were so excited about their colour profiles and wardrobe plans that they brought in nine other members of their family! They ranged in colour groupings from the light brightness of Spring, through the muted Summer to the richness of Autumn and, yes, two of the family turned out to be Winter.

Mimi studies fashion design at college. She is a creative individual who designs clothes and either makes them or has them stitched by others for her ever-growing clientele of executive wives from the diplomatic corps in Japan. Her home reflects her elegance, with pastel pictures in muted violets, blues, rose and green, which pick up the colours used in the interior design. She loves antique silver and is well on her way to an investment which will be cherished by future generations.

Such persons as Margaret and Mimi and other women of

Summer colouring appear softly feminine and fragile and yet they possess a regal quality stemming from an inner strength and dignity. The words 'luscious' and 'luxurious' are used to describe the feminine qualities about her. She may be considered reticent and distant because of her gentle manner and her slight formality. She is sensitive to beautiful things and loves elegance and attention to detail.

It is important that the clothes do not overwhelm the delicate romantic personality of Summer women. The best line for them is the graceful S-curve and the oval shape is also good. These can best be expressed in fabrics that are delicate and sheer or rich and elegant. They should move with the body. If her choice is a floral pattern, they should be tiny cascading flowers such as delphiniums, wisteria, lilies of the valley or trailing roses.

You will see Margaret and Mimi in the colours which are muted as though faded by the summer sun. Picture a grey-blue sky, water that is a muted azure and a garden full of mature roses and other flowers. Think romantic and feminine for the woman of summer colouring. Some of the colours they wear are the American Beauty Rose and cranberry red, moonbeam yellow, eucalyptus and sea green, the blues of blackberries and hyacinths, and purples the colour of iris, amethyst and aubergine. Their neutrals are mother-of-pearl, pewter, rose beige and taupe.

Jewellery for Margaret and Mimi and for women of Summer should not be overdone, especially costume jewellery. Summer metals are silver, platinum or a very soft, rose gold. The Summer women can wear clusters of small stones: stones which flow, rather than sparkle, are best. Margaret has a necklace of five strands of mini beads of rose quartz which are twisted together with a pewter clasp. Precious stones for these women include amethyst, pearl, opal, rose quartz and tourmaline (blue-greens and pink). The women of Summer should achieve a lingering, wafting afterglow in their fragrances to complete the effect.

A very successful financial consultant felt his wife would be interested in working on the project in which we were involved. A time was arranged for an initial telephone conversation. When Catherine rang me, I could sense immediately all the strength, power, and authority behind her. Although I had never met Catherine, I sensed she would be an individual of the Autumn colouring after all I had learnt from Ms Windsor-Williams. When we finally met, she was all I expected – a statuesque, auburn-haired woman who took command as she entered the room.

Catherine had been involved in designing and creating stained glass windows for casinos, homes, restaurants and had just completed a 16 ft high window in a magnificent church. She is dauntless. Catherine has a beautiful Victorian house and is raising three splendid children while supporting her husband in all his varied and demanding business and social affairs. Catherine, being of Autumn colouring, is energetic and dynamic as are all executive wives of similar colouring. She has great drive and intensity, harvesting life abundantly. The Autumn type is sure of her movements, solid and firm of step or quick and wiry. She is a positive, vital woman and often quick to make decisions and say what is on her mind.

The Autumn woman sometimes feels misplaced in a feminine world because she appears more chic than pretty. Autumn executive wives like Catherine have tremendous drive and are never lazy, but are tenacious. They can count on themselves, whatever the odds. The lines of the Autumn woman's clothing should be energetic and swift to complement her vital personality. As the Autumn season reflects the flamboyance of nature, so should the Autumn woman select designs that are strong and flamboyant. She can wear fabrics that look like snakeskins, exotic animals, leather, suede and heavy knobbly textures. Designs reflecting the Chinese culture are also excellent. The Autumn woman should not wear flowers unless they are elegant such as bronze orchids or chrysanthemums. Other designs should reflect the season, such as the leaf, woodsy effects or distinctive geometric designs. Paisley and Persian prints are very good.

The colouring of the Autumn woman demands a brilliance to tone with the earthy hues. She wears colours of spice and hues of topaz, copper, bronze and burnished gold to show off her auburn or red hair. She also wears brick, terracotta red and quince, persimmon, the burnished yellows of chrysanthemum, straw, curry, saffron, and greens of moss, olive and chartreuse, with blues found in jades, Indian turquoise, peacock blue and browns such as tobacco, cafè au lait, cedar. An Autumn woman such as Catherine can wear heavy, ornamental jewellery as lavishly as she wishes. It is the prerogative of Autumns to use jewellery that is as unusual as possible: solid, heavy designs or the bizarre are quite acceptable. Catherine has a necklace with hand-carved wooden beads and exotic animals which is one of her favourites. The Chinese motif is worn well by the woman of Autumn colouring, but is out of place on any other type. The Autumn woman wears metals of gold, bronze or copper very well. Usually, metals without stones are best, but precious stones include jade, topaz, amber and turquoise. The Autumn woman wears well the animal-fixative perfumes which cling to the body for the final and total effect.

I ran across Marilyn at a medical convention in London. She is married to leading plastic surgeon from California. Marilyn is tall, slender and regal with black hair, gardenia skin and spruce green eyes. When she enters a room it is with a dignity which causes all eyes to turn and observe her. She runs her home with perfection and never fails to be an asset while at her husband's side. One of her greatest interests is running a fashionable boutique which reflects her love of the finer things in life. Her favourite colours are the stark black and white and royal purple, holly berry red, crème de menthe green and pure cobalt blue. She has her own 'point of beauty' in her elegant home, where she goes every day to do her creative work and sort out future plans. She sits at a black lacquer Oriental desk with pictures of an ancient emperor and empress. When I told Marilyn that almost everyone of her Winter colouring needed a time to themselves each day and in such suitable surroundings, she delightedly told me about this.

Marilyn, like other women of Winter colouring, is cultured and refined, controlling her life with dignity. Her quiet, self-assured manner, which seems to come from an inner confidence, is sometimes misinterpreted as coldness. Winter's people tend to be perfectionists, having a will of iron and hence make black-and-white decisions. Characteristic of women of Winter colouring is their sense of design which enables them to detect any distortions from the pure line. As in the winter season, you stand in a meadow covered with snow gazing up at a midnight sky with stars sparkling as diamonds and a hush has fallen over the earth, so a woman of Winter colouring appreciates silence. She needs some time spent each day being herself with silence. The lines for the Winter woman should reflect the pure and simple lines such as the oval or draped effect of the S-curve. This woman, who can wear intense and vivid colours, should limit her combination of colours to no more than two, or one colour with a second colour as accent. There should be one area of focus in the clothes of the Winter woman. The adage 'less is more' could never be more true than here. She should always wear garments that are not skimpy. The Winter woman wears abstract or unique designs; never a flowered or 'cute' print. Fabrics best suited for the design line of the Winter woman are soft and flowing or those which are gossamer-like or shot with metallic threads.

Marilyn considers some of her best colours to be poinsettia, ruby and magenta for the reds, champagne for her yellow, pure cobalt blue, royal purple, black olive, gunmetal, silver, dove and new snow white. The jewellery for Marilyn is well defined, simple, large and dramatic. She uses the silver metals best and her stones are precious, clearcut and sparkling. These stones include diamonds, crystals, jets, sapphires, rubies, emeralds and pearls. Marilyn wears lots of jet beads to bring out the natural sparkle she has in her eyes and face. Her husband did not overlook all of this when he gave her an exquisite diamond necklace with matching earrings. Winter women are best complemented by highly sophisticated and distinctive fragrances which are non-floral.

As a result of the profiles I have shared with you, I hope you can begin to identify yourself with a season and apply some of its suggestions for improved results while interacting with others. You can make a proper and educated statement about yourself by choosing the best of fashion in colours that truly reflect and complement you.

As I have already mentioned, the use of colour has definite impact on our perceptions, but most importantly, on the perceptions others have on us. To talk about colours specifically, you may be surprised at the true or implied meanings that have survived from the beginning of time to the present.

Many symbolic uses of red, for example, have arisen from an association with blood and red represents health, tragedy, anger and many attributes more or less allied with such things. Red has symbolised fire, war, destruction, hatred and power. However, it is also an emblem of love and beauty. When red is diluted with white and sometimes blue, resulting in rose and pink, it represents beauty, love and hope. Red has always been a successful colour for me personally in business dealings. My red wool jacket in particular has stood me in good stead for years. Red can be considered a warm colour of great power but when mixed with sufficient blue, it becomes neutral or downright cold. So it is important that you discover your 'power' shades of red and put them to work for you as well.

I was leaving a resort early one morning still feeling sleepy-eyed and yawny, but I swear to you that every single soul who saw me offered an enthusiastic 'Hello, good morning and how are you!' It was unusual in its excessivenes, and especially since I did not appear to welcome the greetings. I wore a cashmere jacket that morning of a yellowish-orange shade. Later, I came to realise that this colour's most striking characteristic is luminosity. The brighter colours represent light and warmth. Yellow is perceived to be gay, lustrous and enlivening. In China, yellow has been quite extensively used as a noble and sacred colour. Further, yellow has the added quality of brilliance which often exemplifies power and glory. Well, I am now surprised that 'hellos' were all I got that morning, next time, I will expect much more!

A good friend of mine loves green above all. Although she is of Autumn colouring, she will wear and surround herself with nearly all shades of green. When she enters a restaurant wearing her favourite fitted Italian silk emerald green dress, she knows forks and jaws will drop. When she puts on a cosy green wool sweater and begins a task, she knows it will be well completed. When she wears her green linen Ungaro suit to a meeting, she is assured of having everyone's focused, undivided attention. Such is the power of this colour once she commands its use. Green mostly signifies youth and vigour. It has also been known to represent hope and victory. And, of course, we all know that olive is a sign of solitude and peace. Green is the colour of spring, thus best representing hope, victory and abundance. It indicates life and thus green becomes the symbol of immortality.

However, in another instance, the wife of a bank manager who had a passion for the colour blue, found herself receiving remarks about her attitude more often than she cared to. This she found particularly distressing since she aimed to please. We discovered that the quality most prominent in blue is coldness. We further learned that it communicates this property in differing degrees to all colours which have blue components. Sometimes blues can be characterised as dignified and calming. As the colour of the sky, it is naturally associated with heaven, hope, serenity, intelligence and honesty. It is a colour reserved for divinity, and supreme intelligence. But blue is also so often associated with coldness and melancholy and with dismal and unpromising prospects; hence, under certain circumstances, it can certainly work against you.

My friend Alexandra on the other hand never had such problems. She spends much of her time living in the vast openness of the green American southwestern desert and is constantly clad in white. I was convinced this was strictly due to weather conditions, but Alex told me that in ancient Roman paintings, Friendship was draped in white and Truth was idealised by women holding lilies. I should have known better than to ask! White is, nevertheless, a symbol of light, purity, innocence, truth and peace. Pope wrote of 'White-robed innocence,' Shakespeare considered it 'As chaste as unsunn'd snow,' and Akenside spoke of 'The snowy wings of innocence and love.' You will know when to make best use of this colour, but white is so often worn with a contrasting colour, especially black. The combination of these two colours has been variously used to symbolise humanity, melancholy, resolution, secrecy and prudence.

Black on its own still manages to conjure up images of gloom, darkness, terror, crime or ill will. You have heard of black sheep, black tidings, Black Friday and, when the stock market crashed, Black Monday. Yet black has another aspect. It is silent, and awakens the imagination. Black combines well with other colours. It harmonises beautifully with the brightest of colours for very effective results indeed.

An associate of mine, who for years was a passionate devotee of black and white and rich bold colours, recently sent me a letter written on the plainest grey stationery. It struck me as unusual for a brief moment, but I paid no attention to it until I saw her some weeks later in her office. She was pale and had an atmosphere of neutrality and tranquillity. Ellen has changed a bit, I thought to myself. But the greys that dominated her appearance lately represent penance, humility, sadness, matured judgement. In nature, grey is interpreted as cool, retiring and suggestive of distance. To the English poet Thomson, grey skies of winter are 'sullen and sad' it is 'leaden dullness.' I learned some time later that Ellen had suffered great personal loss and had a bit of difficulty coming to terms with her newfound realities. Hence, whether consciously or not, her inner being was reflected in the choice of her surroundings.

It has been my experience that conscious observation of colour is important to notice and quite risky to ignore. You may not be particularly aware of your colour selections, but when you are in the company of others – others whose impression of you is important – they may be aware of your choices, whatever they may be, and judge you accordingly. Knowing that you live in a subjective and prejudging society, you have the ability to manipulate the situation in your favour. If you are going to be scrutinised, then you might as well make it be on your own terms. You decide under which circumstances that will be.

As I have shown by these brief, simple examples, association is a very important factor in interpreting colour, like many other things that affect us in life. Becoming aware of these factors will assist you in profiting a little better in your dealings with other people.

10

How to put your best face forward

It was nearly evening on a late Friday afternoon in May when a fuzzy-haired redhead with excessively oily skin stumbled into a Beverly Hills beauty salon on the corner of Wilshire Boulevard and Rodeo Drive. A tape recorder, long microphone chord, portfolio and bags hung from her shoulders as she introduced herself to the elegant, elderly proprietor, Aida Grey.

'You look awful!' Miss Grey said to her.

'Well, I flew in this morning. I did an interview with Randy Gardner and Tai Babilonia over brunch. Then, we went for a meeting in Glendale and stopped by Jay Bernstein's house in Bel Air on the way to meet Dee-Dee Jackson and Nina Field before we . . .'

'You look just awful!' Miss Grey repeated fiercely to the twenty-year-old college student and magazine editor who was there to interview her. But Miss Grey did not give a damn 'why' she looked so awful, she just insisted that she did. She took her to a secluded little room for their interview and shut the door. I am certain that she did not want to discourage any business by having her present in the salon! Miss Grey, who had been responsible for the appearance of Marilyn Monroe, Clark Gable, Betty Grable, Madonna and Barbara Walters, among others, granted the interview providing the girl would come back and be 're-made'. It was a deal.

This was some six years ago and the girl in question is my co-writer of this book. She soon enough grew to admire, respect and befriend the knowledgeable legend in the beauty industry.

Aida Grey has a remarkable way of reaching women and we bring her legendary philosophy to you, the executive wife.

First of all, she believes that a woman must 'create' herself.

'Beauty is the natural state of the whole woman, fully realised. Beauty comes from within. It is a natural part of every woman. And it can be found in any woman who truly seeks it. Nothing can compare with the deep satisfaction and the true sense of fulfilment I have achieved in assisting a woman to pass through the chrysalis stage to emerge as a butterfly. It is a magical moment indeed when a woman realises, perhaps for the first time, that she looks great.'

Miss Grey goes on to explain how that change has many wonderful little ripples, for it affects other areas of your life in an almost tangible way. Feeling confident about your appearance removes a symbolic burden from your shoulders – a secret need to hide yourself – and makes it possible for you to open up to the world. You have seen the woman who feels unattractive. She hides her face with her hands when she talks, or speaks too loudly or rapidly, or simply experiences her irritation with herself and her world as she interacts with others. Watch her after she has begun to develop her attractiveness and you will see a different demeanour, a new openness and freshness. She has faced herself. Now she can move on to face the world.

Psychologists suggest that physical attractiveness and emotional health are closely interrelated, Miss Grey continued, and that has certainly been her experience. An unattractive appearance can affect many aspects of a woman's life, both private and professional, and a depressed person or one with low self-esteem tends not to make herself as attractive as possible – thus perpetuating a cycle of self-defeat. By simply beginning to care for your physical beauty, she says, you have entered a new phase: you are bestowing a gift on yourself, a gift of love. Quickly it will begin to be reflected in your eyes, in your skin, in a new glow and sparkle and a new self-confidence. As your confidence grows, so will your self-esteem. And as you continue your beauty régime, its effects will increase. The changes in your skin will be cumulative, because your skin and your body respond over time to the care you regularly lavish on them. Miss Grey says:

'Of all the thousands of women I have seen and been permitted to help with their cosmetic problems, I have found not one – not one – who did not have at least one beautiful feature. You have at least one. Perhaps it is your eyes or your smile. If it is the warmth of your manner and graciousness of spirit then you already have your greatest asset. Add to these knowledge, compassion, achievement, clever make-up, and a daily routine of thoughtful care, and you will attain the goal.

'You may tell yourself that for you there are better things than the pursuit of "superficial values" such as the exterior beauty of face and form. You have neither the time nor the inclination for such shallow goals, you may say. But be honest – and listen to me for a moment. I have dealt with this attitude more times than I can count, and I have found that it often derives from a profound fear of failure. If I never try, says such a woman, it can never be said that I failed. Nothing can so distort a woman's personality; nothing will so surely thwart full development.

'The truth is this: in the woman who is completely realised as a person, attractiveness of spirit and appearance will be joined. Development in one area will encompass and enhance the other. From this will come a deeper and fuller sense of well-being and confidence. Life will open and extend itself with expanded opportunities. Soon the dream you hesitated to admit to yourself you had, the miracle you longed for, will be yours. In the fullness of the self you have realised you will find the beautiful woman you were meant to be.'

Aida Grey has a precise definition of beauty. She will go as far as to say that beauty is what life is all about! She reminds us that since the beginning of time, the quest for beauty has spurred humanity on to great achievements, great art, great love and happiness. This intangible yet powerful force has cultivated us, made us interesting and complex. And as beauty enters our lives, we are happier, enlightened. Justification is not necessary. As Emerson wrote, 'Beauty is its own excuse for being.' Miss Grey believes that personal beauty is a priceless possession to be realised, cared for and preserved. If abused, it departs. If revered, it becomes a part of the soul and the entire being. True beauty, as she sees it, is so much more than the conventional image of a passive, portrait-like loveliness. It is not defined by the caprices of changing fashion (which inevitably do enhance our appearance) but by the more elusive something that captivates the mind as well as the eye, that touches the heart as well as the visual senses. The woman who captures this 'illusion of beauty' will not fade with the passing years but will actually grow lovelier. She will be ageless. And, she will be beautiful at every age.

'As a beauty scientist,' Miss Grey points out, 'I have been privileged to work with many truly beautiful and glamorous women. Yet I have found working with the so-called plain woman extraordinarily rewarding. Perhaps this is because of an unusual beauty that often shines from within, even when a woman's features are irregular. Great artists have always been fascinated by the face that lacks perfection, yet radiates loveliness. Expression, warmth, gentleness, personal vitality and intelligence, and an inner glow bring to even the plainest face a special and lovely quality – one that can be enhanced still further through proper make-up and skin care.

'If the woman has not developed herself as a human being – whether she is naturally attractive or not – there is no challenge. Of course, I can paint a beautiful mask upon her face, but without expression she will be a vacuous doll.

'Looking your best truly influences how you act, how you feel about yourself, and what you are doing in the world. A feeling of well-being, a confidence and serenity, come to a woman who knows she looks well.'

For Aida Grey, beauty begins at home, within the individual.

'It's your attitude towards beauty that's so important,' she says. 'It's like the positive and negative of a picture. A smile can transform the plainest face to radiance and a frown detracts from the most beautiful soul. That's the important lesson I try to teach the women I work with, whether they come into the studios, are mail order customers we see only once a year, or are in a hospital or prison. Anger is truly the enemy of beauty. Anger is a useless emotion. It's a double-edged sword. That is my first lesson to any woman no matter where she is or what her position may be.'

I knew exactly what she meant when I met Anne. She was the wife of a stockbroker and was actively involved in her own career as a computer analyst. She was dark, vivacious and had a good personality. But she was angry! Her attractive looks were marred by a drooping mouth and a permanent scowl. Her husband had a good position with a well-known firm of stockbrokers and he had worked there for a number of years. He was given the impression by his seniors that he would be next in line for a good promotion. Anne and he spent many hours contemplating how they would spend the extra money he would have and how they would entertain many new clients. But somehow this did not materialise.

One of the senior executives retired early and Anne's husband was interviewed for this position. He seemed to do reasonably well and they both thought it would simply be a formality before he was offered the job. However, the company decided to bring in someone else from outside who had been headhunted to fill the vacant position. Her husband was devastated.

From that moment, Anne became bitter. She blamed the company for not seeing her husband's talents for what she assumed they were. She resented the other executives' wives and their material possessions. She would not take part in any of the corporate entertaining or attend any of the company functions. She made it perfectly obvious to all that she was thoroughly annoyed and angry that her hsuband had been treated in this way. This attitude made her husband react in a way foreign to his own personality both at business and in the home. He and Anne began to have rows during which Anne would upbraid him for being inadequate. She blamed him, it seemed, for not achieving the position she wanted him to have and one which would promote their status. The rows became so bad that eventually her husband decided that he would apply for a similar position in another company and, after many interviews, he was offered a good job with more pay.

But by then, Anne's anger had become part of her outlook. She began questioning her husband about everything he did and accused him of not being intelligent enough for her. To say that their marriage hit a rocky patch was certainly an understatement. Things continued in this way for some time and probably would have gone on but for a chance meeting with a friend who was studying psychology. Over lunch one day, Anne told her valued friend how she felt. She explained how her anger was destroying her marriage. Her friend told her that one of the simple things to do when you feel anger is to release some of it by beating the bed or kicking pillows in a harmless way; this releases pent-up anger, as does playing tennis or running. She had also learnt that many people like Anne could not enjoy their life to the full because they were blaming other people (in Anne's case, her husband) that life was not what they wanted it to be. She went on to say over coffee that we often refuse to realise that holding on to what has happened in the past is hurting us! Other people don't really care or maybe are not even aware. We are only hurting ourselves by refusing to get as much out of life as we can.

Anne listened carefully to what her friend had to say and gradually over the next few weeks, she tried to behave normally towards her husband. Whenever she became angry she would 'fight' the pillows in the bedroom or kick the wall with rage to get rid of the pent-up feelings she had. Her husband knew nothing of this but he was pleasantly surprised at her change of attitude. As time went on and with constant advice from her friend, Anne started to show her true personality again. She began to realise that her frustration over her husband's not getting his initial position had become so intense that all other matters became affected with her anger, and that she herself was suffering both from her attitude and in her looks. She soon began to get back to her normal personality and started to enjoy her life with her husband once again.

Not only are attractive women treated more favourably than less attractive ones, but evidence suggests that people are also more positive towards them in their actions. People are more likely to offer assistance to someone who looks great and to expend quite a bit of effort to win that woman's approval. They will go to great lengths to win her over by being more open, sharing greater intimacies and working harder on an issue or project. The stereotype that better looking women are more socially adept appears to be borne out as well. It appears that attractive women have more frequent social interactions. They possess greater confidence than less attractive peers and they seem to know that their requests and desires will be met.

It is no secret that women in business to-day are usually aware of looking their best at all times during their business day. It is a well-known fact that attractive women can 'open more business doors' than their male counterparts. They can get appointments and are given opportunities that a man would probably have to work twice as hard to achieve. Perhaps attractive women are more confident and assertive because they are used to receiving positive evaluations and feedback from others. Hence, people are more willing to be influenced by opinions and act upon requests that are put forward by such a woman.

11

How to cope with media relations

Public relations are a daily topic of conversation among millions of people. PR is a powerful tool that can assure either success or failure for many politicians, business people, entertainers, athletes, socialites and the like. I cannot think of a single public figure in our society who does not employ skilled public relations personnel. The product of promotion is always oneself. It's a function that evaluates public attitudes, identifies the position and procedures of a person and/or his organisation with the public interest and executes a programme of action to earn public understanding and acceptance. The procedure is quite simple to understand, but often enough it's quite difficult to obtain the desired results for a prolonged period of time. Everyone from John Major to Donald Trump employs public relations specialists to determine three basic objectives: to find out what people think about them; to organise a deliberate campaign to improve or maintain their image; and to use the multiple disciplines and avenues of communications to influence public opinion.

There are those who recognise the desirability of good public relations but maintain that it is something that thrives best when left alone. Personally, I am doubtful, but this may have been true in simpler times. In today's competitive society, good work can no longer speak for itself. Even Mother Teresa understands this! An effective public relations programme allows you to cut through all that static and uproar and deliver your message and present your image clearly to the people who are important to you. Public relations works through an ongoing long-range effort designed to build favourable public attitudes for your position, profession or organisation.

So it is not only love and money that make the world go round, but public relations as well. As an executive or political wife, you are automatically in the business of communication. You are an extension of your husband's profession, firm or government post. Whether by choice or not, periodically you find yourself involved with communicating decisions, making speeches, dealing with the mass media. Although such efforts on your part are commonly viewed as something everyone can do, a quick glance at business, politics and our society in general shows that this is far from the truth. Numerous disastrous outcomes are a direct result of poor communication and image projection. Public criticism of business practices and their disapproval of government action is too frequently due to a communications problem. Those who fully understand our society, realise that absolutely no one is exempt from continuing public scrutiny. Your understanding and use of public relations techniques allows you and your public to function positively and harmoniously.

Why does one person have an excellent reputation among the public while another in a seemingly similar position and status suffers enormously? Richard Branson, the entrepreneur, demonstrates how good public relations can assist in all business matters. His record empire, Virgin airline, and his other numerous projects are constantly in the news. He was seen to mastermind the 'Tidy Up Britain' campaign some years ago which gave him a great deal of good publicity, whilst his daring air balloon journey over the Atlantic kept most of us on the edge of our seats until the event was over. He is always being seen in the presence of influential people both in the business and political world. He is happy to be interviewed on environmental issues, and when it was announced that the hostages from Baghdad would probably be allowed home prior to the beginning of the Gulf War, he and his airline were first in line to bring them and their families back home. These actions are very generous and the hostage families are eternally grateful for his help. Nevertheless, they also ensure that both Richard and his airline are kept well in the forefront of the news, which is very good for his business.

But, as always, when a businessman is put into the public limelight for either good or bad reasons, the wife of that executive has to be extremely cautious over her every move. It is not an exaggeration to say that if a high-profile businessman's wife acts in a way which alienates the press, then this could undo all the good work which he and his company have accomplished – such is the pressure of being an executive wife! Similarly, of course, the wife has to suffer when her husband has done something to alienate the City and/or the press, and we shall deal with this later.

Meanwhile, let me tell you about Karen. She was married to an entrepreneur who had made his money in developing a huge chain of retail stores. His reputation, it seemed, was second to none and the City as well as the press courted him regularly for his views, and at the time he was very well respected by both. The marriage was a quiet affair and was not leaked to the press until it was all over. Imagine everyone's surprise when the press suddenly announced that they were separating after only two months of being married. The press had a field day! For over seven days, they were at Karen's door ruthlessly pressurising her to give some comment, her account of why the marriage had failed.

We received many desperate calls from her during this ordeal and we told her that on no account should she give any interviews whatsoever. Her husband was likewise being bombarded with questions from the press as to why the marriage had seemingly failed. Suddenly, his whole business reputation seemed to be under scrutiny and his financial deals questioned. His plans were to make his company go public that year, but this incident apparently made the City unsure of his credibility. The press interviewed some of his staff, both those still with him and some whom he had fired. Stories of how ruthless in business he was became news; editorial comment was made, especially in many of the more down-market daily papers judging his morals and indeed his sexual preferences! The whole affair became grossly out-of-hand and all the goodwill he and his company had achieved over a decade of business simply appeared to crumble.

Karen had been his secretary for many years and it was no surprise to hear that after divorcing his first wife they were to be married. What was so surprising was, that after such a long friendship, it should end in such a short marriage. We were told by Karen much later that it was her decision to part, but obviously we never knew the reason why. Suffice to say, however, that Karen dealt admirably with the press when she eventually had to face them. She simply said that there were 'insurmountable' differences between them which led to their separation and eventual divorce. After a few months, she left Britain to start a new life in America. When last I heard of her, she was doing well in establishing a modelling agency in Chicago.

So, as an executive or political wife, you will undoubtedly be bombarded with promotion, media relations, publicity, corporate relations, lobbying and corporate affairs, among others. You deal with many different levels of communication at different times in your role. In today's mass media world, public relations is an enormous job, utilising many methods and techniques of communication. But instead of focusing on the overall aspects of useful public relations, I wish to pay attention to you specifically and how you may better perform your job when called upon to do so. I must warn you, however, that how you view public relations has a major impact on how you see your role in the whole process. Public relations pressures are somewhat different from other business expectations. Often, it is not clearly defined what exactly is expected of you, apart from magic. The greatest pressure is the difference between what is possible and what is magic. But if you have put to use the advice offered in the previous chapters, you have a head start among the competition. You are prepared to communicate one-to-one, in small groups, interviews or even news conferences.

When women participate in our Executive Wives seminars, we simplify the situation by outlining initial communication skills. First of all, we write up a description and rationale for focusing on prescribed behaviour. Next, we role-play how to carry such actions out. Then, we offer constructive criticism on each performance and offer alternatives to the situation. Finally, the executive wife, armed with such communication advice, actually carries out the process in a real setting. Each woman has a goal she needs to accomplish. We then outline the procedures and I have her full commitment that she will follow through. We analyse and role-play effective ways of interacting in various business-social situations. We proceed in such a manner that the wives can adopt each practice for their own specific use. One important aspect in functioning successfully is the use of the woman's imagination. She anticipates what may arise and we apply effective social skills to counter-attack the situation.

Judy is the wife of a millionaire banker, and as such she is constantly being requested to give interviews on her way of life to the various women's magazines and some national newspapers. She has all the trappings of a luxury life with a London town house, a country home, 'his' and 'hers' Bentleys, plus a château in Switzerland. One of her main difficulties when giving such interviews is that no matter what she says about the other side of her life, her enormous efforts with charity work, or that both she and her husband regularly donate large sums of money to their local hospital, her interviewers always write about her as 'a rich bitch'. This has happened so many times that she now refuses any such interviews for fear of what they may say next. It emphasises the fact that we in this country, unlike America for example, do not respect wealth. The general view, it seems to me, is that we seem to associate huge wealth with bad taste, or that it has been accumulated by devious means. However, I digress . . .

Judy was very distressed at the last article written about her in a national newspaper giving this same viewpoint and although she felt that she would no longer do any interviews at all, she came to us to see what, if anything, we could do to help her. Initially, we requested that she let us know when other interviews were asked of her. Next, we set out a number of role-playing interviews in which these sort of questions would be asked, and gave her assistance and suggestions on how to reply. For example; 'How much does your husband earn in a year?' is a typical question she would be asked. We suggested Judy should reply as follows: 'I really don't know, my husband doesn't discuss his salary with me, but I do know our hospital wants to extend its maternity wing this year, and he is hoping to be able to donate enough to get this achieved.'

'Do you take long holidays during the year?' To which Judy would reply 'Heavens no! My husband works far too hard for us to take time out for holidays. Besides, this would interfere with my own charity work.' And so on . . .

By matching each innuendo with another, Judy would block any conversations which would lead to the interviewer's possible interpretation that 'I'm extremely rich, I have a wonderfully easy life and take as much time off for leisure as I can!'

We also suggested to Judy that she be very selective with her interviews and establish right from the start why they wanted the article, and what their objectives were. By determining these, she could then decide which ones would be more suitable for good public relations. We went on to back this with a campaign whereby we sent photographs to the press of Judy actively involved in her charity work for children and with press releases stating what she had achieved, emphasising that it was her untiring work and not her money which had brought assistance. Now, whenever she is requested by the media to do any interviews of any description, we analyse each one for her and give useful feedback as to the success of her carefully controlled comments.

Most of the time, our executive wives are taught to work gradually from simple to more challenging business-related functions. This way they can successfully monitor their progress. The follow-up sessions that provide constant feedback and on-going polishing become something the women look forward to after being able to measure their continued success.

I find that some women perform flawlessly on a one-to-one basis, but experience difficulty when a group is present. Whether such anxiety is due to actual failures under such circumstances or is caused by imagined fears of fumbling, it truly causes enormous difficulties when it comes to dealing with other people. These women I encourage to perform self-relaxation skills. Then of course, I encourage them to employ these newly-learned skills in social interactions. The idea is to use the first signs of anxiety as a cue to warn yourself to relax.

Fear, as you know, can do terrible things to us. We can feel physically sick, our palms begin to sweat, our pulse rate quickens and we can be short of breath. But the adrenalin which fear or anxiety produces can be used in a positive manner. It can assist us to produce better results and can stimulate our thought process. Actors often experience enormous bouts of fear prior to appearing on the stage. Fear or anxiety can also be with us when applying for a job interview. Similarly, it can help us when we are faced with coping with certain situations which wives may well find themselves in. At our courses, we try to imagine that fear descending upon us when perhaps we are suddenly faced with an issue, that simply by being married to a man in the public eye we are expected to deal with and to deal with well.

Fear, like pain, however, is easily forgotten. So we role-play certain situations which could happen which would produce fear for many of us. You are suddenly asked to do a speech at your husband's company dinner, for example. You are asked to represent him at a national function because he is abroad on business, or you have to entertain an overseas client on your own for the same reason. By recognising the fear some of us are experiencing in having to carry out such duties, we must first remember three essential things:

1 Action overcomes fear

2 Learn to relax to overcome anxiety

3 Utilise adrenalin to bring about effective results.

When we experience fear, it is necessary to analyse exactly what we are fearful of. Let's imagine we are asked to make a speech – is it because we do not like speaking in public? Are we afraid of making a fool of ourselves and if so, in what way? Do we know what to say or how to say it? This is when action is required. Once we have established that there is simply no way out of making this particular speech – we have given all the excuses and they have been refused – then first we must find out exactly what the objective of the dinner is and why it is so essential to have a speech from the wife of the chief executive. Once the main aim is established, then we can proceed.

Let us again imagine that the company's main wish is to give a dinner for the executives and their wives as a special 'thank you' for the wives' support and for putting up with many days or weeks when their husbands were away on business. It then becomes clear that you, as the wife of the top man, must reply to the speech prior to yours which will be from your husband's colleague, in which he is required to make 'A toast to the ladies.' You then realise that your speech must be to thank him and also to make suitable comments regarding the fact that because your own husband has been away so often, you have now developed so many extra skills, such as mending a fuse or changing a tyre on the car, that you don't need him anyway!

So your action has established that you now know the purpose of the event and what you would like to say. Next you have either to write the speech well in advance yourself or use a professional consultancy to write it for you. Once the speech is prepared, you should go over it time and time again until you feel word-perfect. You will find that once you have become involved in this type of action, some of your initial fears will be somewhat subdued.

Next you have to learn to relax. Leading up to the speech and during it, you have to be able to use methods to control the panic or fear within you. During the weeks and days prior to the speech, use the mirror method (which I have already explained in previous chapters). Look at yourself in the mirror and say 'I *will* do my speech well.' To some, this idea sounds too funny for words, but I can assure you that it works. By confirming this message in your own subconscious, you will be given added strength and will find that your speech will be better than you ever thought. Keep repeating this message whilst you are doing your chores; ironing, taking the children to school, shopping. 'I *will* do my speech well!' By saying this and believing it, you will begin to have more and more confidence, which will remain with you.

On the evening of the function, whilst you are getting ready, breathe very deeply whenever you begin to feel anxiety. Take more deep breaths, and as you exhale, allow all the tension to leave your body. Let your scalp and your forehead, as well as your face, relax. Let your tongue and your throat and your shoulders relax. Now let your back and your abdomen and your pelvis relax. Let your breathing become slow as you relax your legs and feet. Go over this exercise two or three times and by doing so you begin to feel a sense of calm. Make yourself let go and repeat it whenever you feel your negative thoughts of difficult arising.

Take time by yourself to go over in your mind what you have already established. You have prepared your speech. You know what you are going to say. You have identified with your husband that the content is right. You begin to feel good in your new outfit and you know that with your hair and make-up done, you also look good. It is essential to talk your way through each of these items as, by doing so, your confidence begins to return.

Finally, when approaching the venue of the dinner, you naturally will begin to feel again a feeling of fear; anxiety, I would prefer to call it. Learn to relax, knowing that this anxiety can be nothing but good. You know that it will spur you on, so that your speech will be delivered with extra vitality, with extra enthusiasm, so don't be afraid of it. Just before your speech, learn to take long, slow breaths. Breathe in slowly, holding on to that breath for as long as you can and then letting it go again. Do this as many times as you wish. No matter who is sitting either side of you, simply 'switch off' for as long as it takes you to calm yourself down.

You will make a superb speech, your husband's colleagues will say this is only what they expected from you and the press will write favourably about you. After all your hard work, you will be able to enjoy the rewards of doing so, knowing that you have done a job well.

Remember the three principles and ensure that you go through each one of these when faced with any situation which produces fear for you.

1   Action overcomes fear

2   Learn to relax to overcome anxiety

3   Utilise adrenalin to bring effective results.

Many high profile wives are courted by the media as well. Often, the topics of conversation are related to their husband's profession; at other times personality profiles are conducted on the women themselves. Some wives try to shy away from such an involvement, others eagerly anticipate each such opportunity, but whichever the case, your duty is to come across as knowledgeable, intelligent and interesting. Otherwise, you can do more harm than good.

Some executive, political or celebrity wives, when doing an interview learn the hard way that they should have done more to prepare themselves for the opportunity to present their point of view to the public through the media. As many wives will already know to their cost, their own lives are turned upside-down when their husbands are publicly criticised. They will undoubtedly be hounded by the press at all times. When the husband has put a public foot wrong, inevitably the press turns to his wife to pressurise her into difficult situations, so as to make her react either by actions or words. It is at this time that wives have to tread with extreme caution. Everything they do during this time must be thought out carefully and they must establish what is the best way of approaching it. This applies to normal, simple acts such as shopping and taking the children to school. Even the safety of one's home is sometimes at risk.

Koo Stark knows all about press hounding. For months, journalists camped outside her home watching her every move and had infra-red camera lenses so as to endeavour to track her movements in her home at night. One journalist even bought a ladder and climbed up to her bathroom window whilst she was having a bath! Such was her turmoil that after many years of this unpleasantness, she has recently written a book with photographs of other people who have had to endure this enormous pressure. It is no coincidence that she has called the book *Survivors*. In it, you will read of the huge pressure that is put upon someone who is 'wanted' by the press.

The wives of Ernest Saunders and Gerald Ronson during the highly publicised 'Guinness Affair' showed how differently wives cope when disaster hits. Unfortunately, the wife of Ernest Saunders could not take the horrendous publicity in the very early days and had a mental breakdown. We are told she is still recovering in a Swiss hospital and will probably never be the same again.

The wife of Gerald Ronson was, it seems, able to handle her husband's part in the ordeal very well. At his trial, for example, she arrived each day in a different outfit, beautifully groomed and smiling at the cameras. However much the press tried to make her talk to them, she would smile elegantly and say 'No comment'. Her pain at being in the public eye in this terrible way, and her tears, were no doubt only allowed to show in the safety of her own home.

I have mentioned Margaret Thatcher many times in previous chapters, as I am a fan of hers, but now I would like to mention her husband Denis. He has, throughout her term of office, been the perfect 'corporate husband'. During her difficult times when it seemed all the world was against her, at the beginning of the Falklands War, her apparent 'obstinate' views on the European monetary issues and finally when her own party voted her out, Denis remained, in public at least, calm and unruffled towards the press. However – and here is the point that all us wives should remember – he was the real strength behind her. He was the one to whom she turned when she needed reassurance and a comforting arm round the shoulders.

It is vital that you understand that as the wife of a man who is at the top of his profession, both you and he become public property. It is therefore wise to train yourselves to cope with any media situations which may occur. You must remember that an interview is not a conversation. It is a ritual in which the journalist represents the public and your answers and comments are directed to the public through the media. You are being interviewed because a publication wants to sell copies or a programme wants good ratings. Don't be fooled into thinking that the reporter is there to flatter or favour you. He is a professional with a specific job to do. You are his subject at the moment. Since both of you have gathered to perform a duty, you also need to be prepared for the task at hand. You, too, have some research to do. It is difficult enough to remember everything about your activities when you are not under pressure. Imagine how much more challenging it could be under a stressful situation. Take the time to bring yourself up to date on current issues as they affect you, recent news stories about your husband's company or industry or matters relating to your personal interests that you wish to express. Of course, you should always anticipate key questions. Areas of potential interest, hot topics or controversies will not be ignored by the reporter.

Liz found this point out rather suddenly and was thrown into the public eye before she knew what was happening to her. As the wife of the head of a small building company, she was delighted for him when he told her that he had gained a contract to build most of an industrial park in a suburb just outside Manchester. He was over the moon at achieving this, which was undoubtedly the biggest contract he had ever dealt with. The industrial park was to be built to house large manufacturing plants, warehouses and showrooms, as well as blocks of offices. It would take months of work to establish exactly where the buildings would be best situated and much discussion took place with architects as to how this should be done. When the plans were initially shown to the local press, however, events took a turn for the worse. Apparently environmentalists objected to that particular part of the countryside being dug up and virtually destroyed in order to accommodate such a project. They implemented a campaign to lobby industrialists and environmentalists alike to have the plans vetoed.

People from every walk of life were seemingly pressurised to take part and, of course, very soon the press began talking to Liz. How did she like the idea of the countryside being torn up? Did she not feel badly about the obvious outcome of such a situation? Could she influence her husband to make a stand against it? From being a housewife and mother of two children, she was suddenly portrayed by the press either as one of the instigators of the destruction of the peace of the countryside or, alternatively, as the only person who could influence her husband against the idea. Small wonder she wanted some help!

First of all, we had to establish whether she *did* want to become more involved in this matter. If not, then the simplest answer for her would be to refuse all interviews. Once she confided to us that she now wanted to pursue this, we set up her and her husband with a series of some twenty questions which were to be answered by them in front of our television. Even if they had many radio or press interviews, the fact that they could cope with these in front of a televison screen would make them stronger. Our questions would be full of innuendoes, queries and tricks which would be likely to lead them into dangerous situations. One by one we went through the questions and how they should deal with them. We explained how they should respond in such a way that they would sidetrack the main issues but still appear to answer the questions. Let me explain . . .

How often have you noted that politicians avoid answering direct questions? When faced with questions which demand a simple 'Yes' or 'No', they will go off in a different direction and thus avoid the main issue. More aggressive interviewers will still press for a definite reply, but in the main, they are eager to put a further question forward. Using this same technique, Liz and her husband discovered they could similarly avoid the more obvious replies also.

'Mrs Brown, why are you and your husband set to ruin our countryside?' might be a typical example of the line of direct questioning. However she responded to this direct question would be liable to get her into trouble. We suggested she replied, 'During the last two years statistics have shown that the local level of unemployment has risen by 80 per cent. My husband's aim is to bring industry into the town once again so that a large number of people can have a job.'

'But at the expense of the countryside,' the interviewer could reply. 'My husband has made special plans to plant five hundred trees around the project, and each building within the park will have landscaped gardens round it.' And so on . . . Do you get the idea?

This was a serious issue for poor Liz to take on, but take it on she did and overall handled it quite well. Most of us, fortunately, will not have such a serious situation to deal with but it is important to know how to deal with it if it occurs.

So far, it appears that the entire situation is controlled by the media. But naturally, you have some say-so in the process as well. You mutually agree when and where the interview is to be conducted and how much time will be allocated to it. You should request in advance the topics for discussion, and naturally you set the pace for answering them. You can challenge facts and assumptions and sources of information about which you are uncertain.

Now that you are ready to begin, make your interview worthwhile. Deliver your key answers, quotable quotes and anecdotes. Remember to listen very carefully and to speak only for yourself and not on behalf of anyone else. Should the reporter manage to anger you, control the emotion at all costs! Should you be perceived as argumentative by the reporter, it is *your* negative nature, not his, that will show up in the press. You should take all the time you need to state your point to make yourself perfectly understood. You should not be evasive, because it is a signal to the reporter that you may be hiding something. If you are positive and not defensive, you will avoid any temptation to attack someone else or their company, performance or decision. It is also best to plead ignorance to a direct or leading question and offer an informed response to the reporter later so to spare yourself any unnecessary future embarrassment.

The journalist has the advantage of experience over you. She may conduct more interviews in one month than you will give in a lifetime. But you have the advantage of knowledge. I can assure you that a reporter will never know as much about you or your husband as you do!

12

How to play your role in the business-social setting

Your husband is an ambitious, diligent, determined and result-orientated man who ranks at a managerial level. Possibly, he worked his way up the corporate ladder from humble origins or he was one of the young, bright, promising individuals who was the object of an intensive 'headhunt' for executive material. His self-confidence arose from his experiences and capabilities, allowing him to possess the knowledge that he had intelligence, ability and determination to meet the challenges and responsibilities of his company's criteria for success. *You* followed him along. You see his organisation as a highly complex, stratified maze. This group of individuals with common interests in the company's progress, attitudes and image work together as a team employed to generate success.

To function smoothly and profitably, his role is to perform each task with precision. When you, as his wife, are obliged to be at his side, it is mostly in a role that shows you are eager to please, ready to respond and willing to accommodate yourself to the professional philosophy of the organisation. Operating intelligently and exhibiting proper behaviour will only yield greater success for both of you.

In a recent survey by the British Institute of Management it was noted that 81 per cent of the nearly eight thousand top executives who participated were married, or re-married – with 12 per cent single and 7 per cent divorced or separated. It is now acknowledged by most companies that a single man who wishes to reach the top will improve his chances by gaining a wife. In days gone by, the wife did not officially assist her husband, at least not publicly, within his corporate function. History has proved, however, that even in those days when wives were not seen, some of them had a great deal of influence where their husbands were concerned.

Nowadays, wives have been 'promoted' to take a very active part in their husbands' company business. Officially, British companies hotly deny that a man's marital status might be the most persuasive item on his cv. Some say that the concept of a corporate wife is not an integral part of their forward planning, whilst others are appalled at the very suggestion that their employees may be promoted on more than their own personal merit! However, unofficially, other companies will admit that a complete corporate career requires a wife. 'We may not exactly interview the wife, but we make sure she comes out to dinner before we finalise the offer,' said an executive. 'You can't get above a certain rank without a wife who is good at being part of the company,' says another. In America, things are quite different: the husband and wife very often go to the interview for his position together.

Your role today is certainly quite different from that in times gone by when conservative theorists assigned women an unquestionably inferior status. The leaders used to take their stand from the teachings of St Paul, which exhorted the wife to be a crown to her husband, to dress modestly, obey her husband's superior judgement in all matters and find self-expression only in bearing children. But most of all, there was practically an oath of silence placed upon women. The oath was sometimes broken, as witnessed by this brief biographical inscription on granite:

> Here lies as silent clay
> Mrs Arabella Young
> Who on the 21st May
> 1771
> Began to hold her tongue

If you behaved as if you had taken an oath of silence today, the world would not necessarily eye you with admiration. Today a woman is almost expected to be a master communicator whenever she is associated with a successful individual, as well as possessing many other talents. Many wives who are company wives to top executives well believe they are 'married to the company' and accept this as part of their life. Some have careers of their own, while others are content to be brought in whenever there is a reason for doing so.

Jean, who is married to the chairman of a well-known motor company, says his company understands that 'two heads are better than one!' She, meanwhile, feels that it makes sense that the two of them work together to achieve their main aims, which include her husband being a success at what he is doing in the commercial world.

It is clear that if you are a corporate wife, then it is your choice as to how you are going to deal with it. If you don't like the idea and reject it totally, so be it! Many wives have done this and the husband has to accept the situation. He will endeavour to deal with all his business activities outside the home and you will not have to put up with being 'brought out' for high days and company functions. The secret of the success of this, it seems to me, is to discuss it fully with your husband, so that both of you agree and know exactly the position right at the outset. He, however, will possibly be away from home much more, while you are left free to pursue your own life and ambitions. Many couples have made this way of life work very well.

If, however, you decide to become part of his business life, then it is far better to make this decision early and to tackle the situation head-on. Try to become one of the very best executive wives there is. If you like, become obsessed with being known as the brilliant wife of so-and-so. It is true to say that, with few exceptions, most well-known, high-flying executives have wives who back them all the way. They are well presented, well informed and act as perfect hostesses. Even though some people might say that it is a pity some of them have given up good careers in order to devote their lives to their husbands, it has been their choice to do so and the rewards are often great.

The only woman on the board of a financial company, Samantha also assists her executive husband and believes herself to be a corporate wife. She spends all her working days at her own career and is prepared to entertain, when necessary, on her husband's behalf. Quite often, however, they combine forces and have clients from both their respective companies. The one stipulation she makes is that they have good holidays away together and at least one weekend a month is spent with just the family.

'It makes a lot of sense to work out a plan whereby we can both happily do the things we want to do,' she says. 'I am quite content to be his corporate wife when required, as long as he does the same for me sometimes. The only thing is,' she goes on, 'when both of us are working, who does the cooking?'

Janet is different from Samatha. She is very much a company wife and spends all her time involved in her shipping executive husband's business affairs. A bubbly extrovert, she enjoys the trappings that being the wife of a high-flyer brings. There are many like her. She has a beautiful London house near Regent's Park with a perfect yellow and cream drawing room. Tea is poured from a silver teapot. She loves clothes and spends about £6,000 a year on them, shopping in the most famous and expensive boutiques and stores in the world. Recently, she had been buying clothes for their move to the United States. She delights in taking clients to opera and ballet, presiding in the company marquee at Wimbledon, and entertaining clients at the Ritz. She recalls with delight the night she met Princess Anne at a costume ball at Blenheim Palace.

'The other side is that you are married to someone who "lives his job",' she explains. 'He works thirteen hours a day, taking difficult decisions, then he gets stuck in a traffic jam. When he finally gets home he is exhausted and wants to shut off. *You* want to talk'.

Janet has three children, two sons and a daughter, all in their teens and finds that at times they desperately need to see their father. Meanwhile, she has to cope with all the teenage problems on her own. 'There are still some things that fathers should talk about with their sons alone, but I seem to have been landed with the job instead!' She is aware of the pampered image women like her possess. Not only so-called friends, but members of her family, resent her and feel jealous about her way of life. The reality is that wives like Janet have very little private life. The evening at home for dinner for two becomes a rarity, and often husbands are away for long spells at a time. This is particularly so in Britain where, even though company wives are encouraged a great deal more than they used to be, they are still not expected to travel too much with their husbands to meetings abroad. It is different in America, where wives go everywhere with their husbands if they choose to do so.

'People think my life is all champagne and caviar but in real terms it often means a boiled egg at home and an early night,' says Janet. 'My husband seems to be exhausted so much of the time and we can never seem to get enough time alone or have long holidays, unlike the common perception of life of a high-powered man.'

Janet's current problem is that she has to arrange a new life in America. This means that she will see even less of her children as they will be at boarding school. She intends flying back to Britain once a month, which is quite a feat as she hates flying!

No one can quantify the worth of a corporate wife. New-style bosses believe the right wife creating the right ambience can genuinely oil the wheels of business. Cynics say the present trend to include wives is simply a way of keeping the ladies happy. Many would disagree with this opinion. Harrods, the world-famous London store, has recently begun an Executive Service for wives. Situated in the middle of the designer section, Julia will give you all the advice you need on what to wear for any corporate occasion. Her wonderful knack of putting a jacket with a different skirt can transform a suit. She encourages you to be a little more daring with style and different colours. She will plan your wardrobe right the way through, incorporating the main outfit, the hat, plus all the other accessories: all to make you feel a million dollars, whatever your budget! Julia has many company wives who visit her for advice and she maintains that the average wife is still unsure of the role she has to play and feels very intimidated. 'They come to me for wardrobe advice and end up discussing how to cope with the pressures that are being put upon them.'

I read recently that the wife of a company director 'deplores' the idea of a wife being seen as an accessory to a man's career and thinks working women are much more of an asset because they have more to talk about.

A cosmetic consultant told me some time ago that many company wives visit her for advice. She listens to their fears and worries about attending a company function or entertaining clients. She explains that through the power of make-up, she can make any woman feel more confident. She also has to take this role herself beside her merchant banker husband, so she knows what she is talking about!

Quite obviously there is still a long way to go before, firstly, wives are accepted by their husband's companies as an integral part of their forward planning. Secondly, wives themselves are still not certain that this is the role they wish to play or indeed how to play it.

It must be said that a good percentage of younger wives are now taking the initiative and are going ahead with being a 'good company wife'. They realise that if they have not got the skills required already, these can be learned, often by trial and error. If they try on their own to acquire these skills, sometimes the results can be disappointing. If they learn with professionals, then hopefully their mistakes will be fewer.

Many older women obviously find this step a little harder to take. When they first began married life, they were expected to stay at home, cook, sew and clean as well as bring up a family. After many years of this way of living, it becomes very difficult suddenly to emerge into the limelight; to be an extrovert and to be an excellent conversationalist. No wonder many baulk at the idea! My view, however, is that if we decide to become an executive wife then, as with any other executive position, we must work hard and earn the respect we deserve. We know now that we can find advice on the skills we require and ways to make us look and feel confident. A company executive will spend long hours and often 'burn the midnight oil' in order to achieve his ambition, to gain that one extra deal. We must be prepared to do the same. Only by making a supreme effort will we get it right. Acquiring skills to help us improve ourselves in order to fit the role society has allotted to us will make us feel and act in a better way. How we implement those skills is entirely up to each of us individually. We must always be ourselves. It doesn't matter if your best friend is an extrovert and is the centre of attraction at all company affairs. You will be just as respected, just as well liked, by being simply yourself, even if this means you are quiet and do things at your own pace.

An executive wife is one who will be noted for doing her best at all times, for being on top of her 'position', one who can be relied upon to do her job well and is well respected by men and women alike. A friend commented recently about a colleague's wife: 'She's good! She's executive material!'